BERLITZ®

P9-EDC-511

HELSINKI
and Southern Finland

1991/1992 Edition

By the staff of Berlitz Guides

Berlitz Trademark Reg. U.S. Patent Office and
other countries – Marca Registrada.
Library of Congress Catalog Card No. 79-92937

Printed in Switzerland by Weber S.A., Bienne.

5th Printing
1991/1992 Edition

Updated or revised 1990, 1989, 1984, 1982

How to use our guide

- All the practical information, hints and tips that you will need before and during the trip start on page 102.
- For general background, see the sections Helsinki and the Finns, p. 6, and A Brief History, p. 12.
- All the sights to see are listed between pages 23 and 84. Our own choice of sights most highly recommended is pinpointed by the Berlitz traveller symbol.
- Entertainment, nightlife and other leisure activities are described between pages 85 and 94, while information on restaurants and cuisine is to be found on pages 95 to 101.
- Finally, there is an index at the back of the book, pp. 127–128.

Although we make every effort to ensure the accuracy of all the information in this book, changes occur incessantly. We cannot therefore take responsibility for facts, prices, addresses and circumstances in general that are constantly subject to alteration. Our guides are updated on a regular basis as we reprint, and we are always grateful to readers who let us know of any errors, changes or serious omissions they come across.

Text: William Davis
Photographer: Peter Solbjerghøj
Layout: Doris Haldemann
We wish to thank both the Finnish Tourist Board and Kaarina Turtia for their help in the preparation of this guide.
Cartography: 🅕 Falk-Verlag, Hamburg.

Contents

Cover picture: Senate Square (Helsinki)
Photo, pp. 2-3: Olavinlinna (Savonlinna)

Helsinki and the Finns

Helsinki calls itself the "Daughter of the Baltic", and rightly so, for the large northern sea provides the lifeblood of Finland's capital. The city grew up around its harbour and behind the island-fortress of Suomenlinna, gradually expanding into today's metropolis, with its innovative architecture and visionary satellite towns.

Half a million people live in Helsinki, the indisputable centre of Finnish commerce and cultural life. But in spite of its size and sophistication, the city preserves many of the customs and all of the charm of a small 19th-century seaport.

An open-air market is held year-round on South Harbour quay, where seagulls vie with shoppers at stalls piled high with freshly caught Baltic herring and newly dug potatoes. Ferries bound for Sweden,

West Germany, Poland and Estonia are the floating backdrop to this colourful and convivial scene, as well as a reminder of Helsinki's commercial importance.

The city takes as its symbol the sea nymph Havis Amanda, immortalized in bronze in Market Square. The statue rises from a fountain that is the centre of *Vappu* festivities, a celebration to welcome spring, held on the eve of the first day of May. The laughter and gaiety will make you wonder about the reputed reserve of the Finns.

Equally joyous is *Juhannus*, the midsummer celebration in June. Houses and cars are decked with birch leaves, and thousands gather on Seurasaari, one of the harbour islands, to sing, dance and watch

All roads lead to Helsinki Market Square, but in far-off Lapland (see page 9) even roads are a rarity.

Finland

Much of the information given below is contained in different sections of our guide, but for your convenience, key facts are grouped together here for a quick briefing.

Geography	Borders on Norway, Sweden and the Soviet Union. Covers 130,128 square miles with 2,760 miles of coastline and 62,000 lakes. *Population:* 4,900,000. *Capital:* Helsinki (500,000). *Climate:* cold winters (Arctic night), mild summers (midnight sun).
Government	Independence declared December 6, 1917. Parliamentary republic headed by an elected president.
Religion	Evangelical Lutheran Church officially recognized (93% of population).
Getting around	Convenient bus and train services operate in Helsinki area. Taxis plentiful, but expensive. Interconnected train/bus/ferry network covers the country. Internal flights frequent and inexpensive. *Approximate distances:* Helsinki–Turku, 165 km., Helsinki–Kuopio, 390 km., Helsinki–Rovaniemi, 835 km.

the lighting of traditional bonfires. The honour of lighting the last and largest, usually an enormous pile of old boats, goes to a young couple married that day. As the big bonfire slowly sinks into embers, the newly-weds take their leave, but many celebrants linger to grill sausages over open fires and have their fortunes told by costumed gypsy women. Midsummer Eve is a magic time, even in Finland's biggest city.

Only in 1812 did Helsinki become the capital of the Russian Grand Duchy of Finland, an event that triggered an unprecedented building boom. The structures centering on Senate Square are typical of the early 19th-century construction, most of which bears the neo-Classical stamp of the Berlin-born architect Carl Ludvig Engel, who looked to Prussia and St. Petersburg for inspiration.

Helsinki's streets are always thronged with people, especially Esplanadi, where shops display the best of world-famous Finnish-designed goods, characterized by simplicity, utility

On Porvoo river bank, examples of wooden architecture, erstwhile salt warehouses, are preserved.

and bold colour. Whether ceramics, glassware, jewellery or textiles, the items on sale are guaranteed to brighten the darkest Arctic night. The harsh winter climate, with up to 19 hours of darkness daily in December, is said to have encouraged the development of the Finns' aesthetic sensitivity.

This, combined with their legendary *sisu*—courage, tenacity and endurance in the face of adversity—sets the Finns apart from their neighbours in more clement latitudes.

Finns love nature and treat it with a care that verges on reverence. For a large city in an industrialized nation, Helsinki boasts a remarkable amount of greenery and open space. Parks dot the harbour islands of Korkeasaari, Pihlajasaari and Seurasaari. Some, like Kaivopuis-

perfectly normal. All new plans, like those for Espoo and Helsinki's new city centre, concentrated around Finlandia Hall and Töölönlahti, take nature into consideration.

But there is more to Finland than Helsinki, especially for the visitor. No one should miss travelling along the lakes of Great Saimaa, Finland's largest inland sea, covering a huge area of 1,694 square miles. This is the romantic Finland every traveller dreams of, where vintage steamers cruise past birch-covered islands with their old summer cottages and little wooden saunas, docking at picturesque lakeside towns like Kuopio. You'll warm to the humour of Kuopio's people and the simplicity of the Karelians. It was they who safeguarded the *Kalevala*, Finland's epic poem, passing it down from generation to generation by oral tradition alone.

to, Hietaniemi and Sibeliuksen puisto, follow the shoreline, while others run inland to connect with the birch and pine forests of the interior. In fact, in winter it is theoretically possible to put on a pair of skis in Kaisaniemi, a park near the main railway station, and ski north for hundreds of miles to Lapland and beyond the Arctic Circle without taking them off. That the dividing line between city and country should be so unremarkable strikes Finns as

Then there is Åland, a group of several thousand islands off the south-west coast. Cycling, walking, swimming and sailing are favourite activities here. Superb medieval churches adorn a lush landscape of oak groves and meadows, gently contrasting with the pine and birch forests of the mainland. Ålanders are among Finland's Swedish-speaking minority. **11**

Distinctive, too, is Finland's Lapland and its resourceful people, just 4,000 of them. For Laplanders, traditional costumes are an everyday reality and the reindeer, the source of life. Lapland scenery varies from the high, bare western hills to the rolling forested country of the east. During the summer, when the sun doesn't set for about 70 days, Lapland is ideal for hiking, and there is an excellent system of trails and huts. The sun glows on the horizon for about 50 days in winter, but doesn't rise. There are those who claim the effect is romantic, and everyone agrees the Northern Lights displays are spectacular.

Spring days are long and snow is still deep, making this the ideal time for cross-country skiing and hut-to-hut "reindeer safaris". But the most unforgettable season is autumn, usually from early September, when the changing leaves seem to set the landscape on fire. The Finns call the riot of colour *ruska*.

Whether you decide to visit Lapland's wilderness or Helsinki's smart boulevards, Åland's medieval churches or the lakeside towns of Great Saimaa, Finland remains one of Europe's least known, least explored but most scenic and stimulating countries.

A Brief History

About the time of the birth of Christ, the primitive ancestors of the modern Finns wandered into Finland. Their slow migration north had lasted many centuries, taking them from the Volga area of Russia. They absorbed indigenous peoples along the way and gradually evolved their complex, subtle and very distinctive language (see p. 24).

The origin of these nomadic hunters and fishers remains a mystery. While they may not be a unique people, only the Estonians, and more distantly the Hungarians, can claim any real kinship. Together they form the Finno-Ugrian family.

The early Finns found the fish-filled lakes and game-rich forests of their new land very much to their liking. The region was inhabited by native Lapps, who had apparently been in residence for thousands of years, and were pushed further north by the newcomers in a migration that carried them from the vicinity of what is now Helsinki to far above the Arctic Circle.

As they have for centuries, Lapps engage in trade of reindeer furs.

Protected on the west by the sea and on the east by swamps, lakes and dense forests, the Finns lived in relative isolation. It wasn't until some time after A.D. 800 that the Vikings (Danes, Norwegians and Swedes) made contact, first raiding and then trading. Since it was easier to sail a longboat across the Baltic than to haul a wagon or chariot through the Finnish forests, Finland was always more subject to influence from Scandinavia.

Enter Sweden

The country's written history begins in the 12th century with the invasion of Sweden's King

Erik IX, who sought to establish trade routes across Finland to the powerful Russian city-state of Novgorod. In his entourage was Bishop Henry of Uppsala, an English missionary anxious to convert the heathen Finns. In 1154, or thereabouts, the two men launched a crusade that over a 200-year period brought both Christianity—and Swedish rule —to Finland.

Bishop Henry was in the process of consolidating the new religion when he was martyred in the winter of 1155. Henry, the apostle of Finland, was revered as the country's patron saint in the centuries before the Reformation.

The Swedes replaced the loose but democratic clan structure of pagan Finland with a formal administration, and they ruled the country through a provincial governor appointed by the Swedish king. Nevertheless, Finland retained semi-independence throughout the Middle Ages, a status that was formalized when the country was declared a Grand Duchy of Sweden in 1581. During this period, the Åland

Since the 13th century a cathedral has stood on this site in Turku.

islands and south-west coast were settled by Swedes.

From the 13th century on, Turku was the acknowledged spiritual, cultural and administrative centre of the country. The bishops of Finland, from their seat at Turku, encouraged a separate Finnish identity, particularly after the Reformation. Lutheranism was introduced into Finland by Mikael Agricola, who translated the New Testament into Finnish in 1548, creating a literary language in the process. Under the Lutherans, Finnish became the language of church services, even when Swedish was the common tongue of the upper classes and the accepted cultural language of the country.

The tiny port of Helsinki, called Helsingfors by its Swedish founders, was not established until 1550, by decree of King Gustavus Vasa of Sweden. He sought to create a commercial alternative to Revel, the Estonian port across the Gulf of Finland, which was controlled by the Hanseatic League. The initial population was so sparse that the king ordered some of the citizens of Porvoo, Ulvila and Rauma to move into the new town, which they did with great reluctance. During the 17th century, Finland became an integral part of Sweden, but retained its own national assembly representing the four recognized social classes: nobles, clerics, burghers, and peasants. Per Brahe, the Swedish viceroy, founded a university at Turku in 1640 and established a court of appeals and town charters.

The Finnish assembly normally convened in Turku, but in 1616 King Gustavus Adolphus II ordered it to meet in Helsinki. No one would ever have guessed that Finland's representatives would one day have Helsinki as their permanent home—or even that Helsinki would survive. The original site by the Helsinge rapids, which gave the town its name, was abandoned in 1640 because of silting. But even in a more auspicious situation in the area now called Kruununhaka, infant Helsinki was beset with troubles. Within five years, fire broke out and three-fourths of the town burned down. Then came the Great Famine, which caused much suffering.

Russian Aggression
The Great Northern War between Sweden and Russia for control of the Baltic broke out in 1700 and lasted for 21 years. Finland, set right between the **15**

Day-trippers take the sun amid 18th-century Suomenlinna fortress, built by Swedes to deter Russians.

two, was the battle ground and found itself ravaged by the conflict. The fate of Helsinki was typical of much of the country, with an epidemic in 1710 decimating the inhabitants, and three years later the retreating Swedish army setting fire to the town.

Russian troops moved into what was left of Helsinki and stayed there until the end of the war. Most of the citizens had fled to Sweden during the occupation, but a handful returned as soon as the war ended, determined to re-build the city; Helsinki slowly revived.

Russia and Sweden fought again from 1741 to 1743, and once more the Swedes fared badly. This time the war worked to Helsinki's advantage: refugees from territories to the east that had been ceded to Russia settled in the town, swelling the population. Most important of all, the Swedes, backed by their allies, the French, decided in 1748 to build a great sea fortress near Helsinki to contain Russia's westward expansion. The construction of Suomenlinna,

did the well-to-do merchants who supplied the fortress, and the population grew to more than 3,000. By 1808, when fighting broke out again between Russia and Sweden, Helsinki boasted nearly a dozen stone buildings. The short-lived war, a complete disaster for Sweden, was waged on Finnish soil. Once more Helsinki was occupied by the Russians, who found the town in ashes, two-thirds of it destroyed by an accidental fire.

From their base in the charred remains of Helsinki, Russian troops laid siege to Suomenlinna, making good use of psychological warfare techniques. They faked the arrival of reinforcements and sent in to the fortress newspapers reporting Russian victories. When the Russians finally advanced over the ice late in the spring of 1808, the Swedish Gibraltar surrendered to a vastly inferior force without firing a shot.

called Sveaborg under the Swedes, ushered in a new era of progress for Helsinki.

The main fortifications of the "Gibraltar of the North" were built on five connecting islands, and the installation included not only military bastions and barracks, but a naval yard and base as well. France financed the fortress, and French officers were involved in its construction. Through them and the brilliant Swedish Admiral Augustin Ehrensvärd, the ideas of the French Enlightenment entered Finland.

Helsinki benefited from all this, of course. Families of the garrison lived in the town, as

Under Russian Rule

The fall of Suomenlinna sealed the fate of Finland—and ensured the future of Helsinki. Under the terms of the treaty that ended the war in 1809, Finland was incorporated into Russia as an autonomous **17**

Grand Duchy, with the czar as Grand Duke. Czar Alexander I proved a liberal ruler. The Finns gained more control over their own affairs than they had under the Swedes, including their own Diet, courts and army.

The czar considered Turku to be too close to Sweden, and in 1812 proclaimed Helsinki capital of the new Grand Duchy. A local committee approved the town plan designed by Johan Albrecht Ehrenström and selected the Prussian architect Carl Ludvig Engel to implement it. Until his death in 1840, Engel worked indefatigably to make Helsinki a worthy capital.

In 1819 the Senate was transferred from Turku to Helsinki. After a fire swept through Turku in 1827, the university was also moved to Helsinki. As the seat of both government and higher education, Helsinki was bound to prosper, and the expanding bureaucracy provided jobs for new citizens. Cultural life developed too, as did Finnish national consciousness.

The Rise of Nationalism
In 1835 Elias Lönnrot, a country doctor and avid folklorist, published the first complete text of the *Kalevala*, the na-

tional epic which had been preserved since pre-Christian times by oral tradition alone. Publication gave tremendous impetus to nationalism and led to the resurgence of the Finnish language and development of a vernacular literature. In 1863 Finnish was finally recognized as an official language.

Throughout the 19th century, Finland benefited from Russia's policy of tolerance and separate development. In 1863 Czar Alexander II summoned the Diet (which had not met for 54 years) to a meeting in Helsinki, ushering in a progressive period of administrative, educational, and economic reform. But at the end of the century, Czar Nicholas II launched a campaign of Russification. Helsinki, by then the economic centre of the nation with a population of nearly 100,000, was in the forefront of opposition to czarist rule.

Russification
In 1899 the Finnish Diet was stripped of its powers; two years later, the Finnish army was abolished. These and other manifestations of Russification by Governor General Nikolai Bobrikov produced petitions, protests and demonstrations. Mounted Cossacks confronted

18

outraged citizens in Senate Square, newspapers were shut down and prominent citizens exiled to Siberia.

The fury of Finnish nationalists finally resulted in the one and only political assassination in Finland's history: Governor Bobrikov was shot in Senate House in 1904. The following year, in the wake of Russia's defeat in the Russo-Japanese War, workers demonstrated for universal suffrage in Senate Square. As in Russia itself, a general strike forced the czarist government to concede reforms.

Finland was granted a democratically elected Diet, and Finnish women became second in the world to gain the right to vote. Nevertheless, Russification remained an official policy. Finland was not directly involved in World War I, but young nationalists were smuggled into Germany to receive military training.

Various opponents of czarist rule sought refuge in Finland, and it was here in 1905 that Lenin and Stalin first met. When Lenin discovered in 1907 that he was under surveillance, he left the country, not to return until a few months before the czar was toppled from power. Lenin advocated the cause of Finnish independence and promised that he would grant the country independence when he came to power.

Independence

But the Finns jumped the gun, declaring independence on December 6, 1917, during the turmoil of the Russian Revolution. This signalled the outbreak of a short but bloody civil war in Finland between the revolutionary-led Reds and conservative Whites.

In January, 1918, the Reds took Helsinki, forcing the new national government to flee. The Whites established headquarters in Vaasa and counterattacked under the leadership of General (later Marshal) Carl Gustav Mannerheim. With the help of a German-trained batallion and the support of Sweden, they slowly re-captured the country. By mid-May Mannerheim became regent of a transitional government, and in 1919 a republican form of government was established.

During the decades between the wars, Finland concentrated on healing social and political wounds and rebuilding the economy. The republican government was practical, devoting most of its revenues to education and economic development.

19

Soviets Attack

Many Finns were to wish that a larger percentage of the pre-war budget had been devoted to defence, when in 1939 Russia demanded territorial concessions in eastern Finland and the lease of a naval base on the south coast. The Finns tried to negotiate an agreement that would satisfy the Soviets without compromising Finnish sovereignty, but that proved impossible.

The Soviet Union renounced its non-aggression pact and on November 30, 1939, attacked Finland, confidently expecting victory within a few weeks at the most. But the Finnish David stood up to the Russian Goliath. The main Soviet thrust was concentrated on the Karelian isthmus, where six Finnish divisions dug in along the Mannerheim Line, named after Marshal Mannerheim, who was now commander-in-chief of the armed forces. The Finns held off more than a dozen Russian divisions and inflicted heavy casualties on the attackers.

Despite the intense cold and heavy snow that made the struggle in every sense the Winter War it came to be called, fighting continued for more than three months, both in Karelia and in the northern part of the country. While the Finns fought with tenacity (many of them on skis), they were eventually overcome by the sheer weight of the forces thrown against them. But not before Finnish troops inflicted heavy casualties on the fatally over-confident Red Army. On March 12, 1940, a peace treaty was signed in Moscow. Under its harsh terms Finland lost about 10 per cent of its pre-war territory, including Vyborg (then Viipuri), the second-largest city.

Inevitably Finland was drawn into World War II, which is known to Finns as the Continuation War. Although pursuing an independent policy, Finland allied itself with Germany and participated in the war against Russia, primarily to recover lost territory. Once that aim was achieved, the Finnish army pursued an essentially defensive strategy. Finns refused, for instance, to participate in the siege of Leningrad. When the tide turned and the German army retreated, while the Soviets took the

Statue in central Helsinki honours Mannerheim, leader of resistance to the Soviet army in Winter War.

offensive, Finland once again stood in the path of the Red Army steamroller.

A Difficult Peace

In September 1944, Marshal Mannerheim—who had become president—sued for peace. Under the terms of the treaty, Finland returned to the post-Winter War borders and lost the Arctic port of Petsamo. Finland also agreed to pay the U.S.S.R. reparations that totalled U.S. $300 million.

In human terms, the cost of the war was immense. Some 80,000 Finns were killed, many wounded and nearly half a million forced from their homes. Physical damage was not as severe as it might have been. Finnish cities were bombed, but none was levelled. The greatest damage to Helsinki was done in a series of air raids in 1944, and retreating Germans burned down Rovaniemi, the capital of Lapland, and nearly all villages.

Modern Times

To provide work and hard currency to meet reparations payments, metallurgical, mechanical and other new industries were developed, almost from scratch. The post-war influx of refugees increased Helsinki's population by about 20 per

Finland and the Soviet Union
A policy of absolute neutrality has enabled Finland to preserve a democratic society in the shadow of the Soviet Union. Finland maintains close ties with the Scandinavian countries, through membership on the Nordic Council, while pursuing a friendly relationship with the U.S.S.R., formalized in the 1948 Treaty of Friendship, Cooperation and Mutual Assistance (renewed in 1970). Finland and the Soviet Union have become trading partners, and they share the administration of the Saimaa Canal. But the treaty does not oblige Finland to come to the defence of the U.S.S.R.

Finland's military strength is the minimum necessary for local defence, and troops and officers participate mainly in United Nations peace-keeping operations.

cent, and the rapid industrialization attracted Finns to the capital from all over the country.

The centre of Helsinki has changed surprisingly little over the years. Because of pressing post-war priorities, no major public buildings were constructed until more than 20 years after the end of World War II. It wasn't until 1967

that the City Theatre was built, and construction didn't start on Finlandia Hall until four years after that.

Alvar Aalto's marble masterpiece demonstrates the renewal and revitalization of Helsinki, and as a venue for international conferences has come to symbolize the unique role Finland has created for itself as a bridge between East and West.

Marble landmark of Helsinki's new centre is Aalto's Finlandia Hall.

What to See

Finland is a small country and its distances are easily covered by the tourist. Most of the population is confined to cities and towns in the south—Helsinki, Tampere, Turku, etc.—leaving large, uninhabited areas that are unique in Europe.

An efficient transport system brings the countryside within easy reach of Helsinki. Boats ply the Lake District, a vast inland sea. Buses and trains cross the plains of Ostrobothnia. Even Lapland, the most remote region of the country, can be visited on a day trip via its gateway capital Rovaniemi, an hour and 40 minutes by jet from Helsinki.

Approximately 30,000 offshore islands and almost 3,000 miles of coastline contribute to the rare natural beauty and variety of the landscapes. Finland is a country to explore, and Helsinki is the most logical starting point.

Helsinki

Most of the sights a visitor should see are concentrated in the compact and eminently walkable centre of Helsinki (museums are normally open between 9 or 10 a.m. and 4 p.m.). Tram and bus lines, as well as ferry and boat services, provide convenient connections to outlying districts.

There is no better way to orientate yourself than a ride on tram 3T. It travels a figure-8-shaped route through the heart of the city, broadcasting a recorded commentary on the sights (except during rush hours).

Start the tram tour at Kauppatori, not far from the Helsinki Tourist Office at Pohjoisesplanadi 19.

Reading the Map

Foreigners are baffled by Finnish—which is understandable, since very few Finnish words have been adopted from other languages, and Finnish itself bears no relation to any major group of languages.

The reason why words are so long is that the Finns indicate number, tense, or whatever by adding a few letters to the end of a word. Moreover, the Finns don't use prepositions, but again add some letters to word endings. Thus "harbour" is *satama*, but "in the harbour" is *satamassa*... A real problem!

However, the language does have one advantage: every letter is articulated and always pronounced in the same way. Words are spelled and pronounced alike, with the accent invariably on the first syllable.

If you keep in mind that ä (like the "a" in "hat") and ö (like "a" in "about") are separate letters with their own sounds, you'll have little trouble pronouncing the terms—and asking for the places—on our maps. Words preceded by the following sign (=) often form the last element of compound words.

=*järvi*	Lake
=*joki*	River
=*katu*	Street
=*kirkko*	Church
=*lahti*	Bay
=*linna*	Castle/Palace
=*museo*	Museum
puisto	Park
=*saari*	Island
=*satama*	Harbour
=*talo*	Hall/Building/House
=*teatteri*	Theatre
=*tie*	Road
=*tori*	Square
tuomio-kirkko	Cathedral

24

On the quay of Helsinki's South Harbour, housewives buy the makings of a typical Finnish meal—new potatoes and freshly caught Baltic fish.

Market Square Sights

The open-air market, held year-round weekdays and Saturdays on **Kauppatori** (Market Square), is at its best early in the morning when stalls are well stocked with fruit and vegetables. Freshly caught fish is sold from boats anchored in Kolera-allas (Cholera Basin), so called because an epidemic of the disease broke out here at the turn of the century.

Stand for a moment amid the flower sellers around the **Havis Amanda fountain,** the symbol of Helsinki, and admire the charming sea nymph by Ville Vallgren that scandalized townspeople when it was placed in the square in 1908.

The genial market atmo-

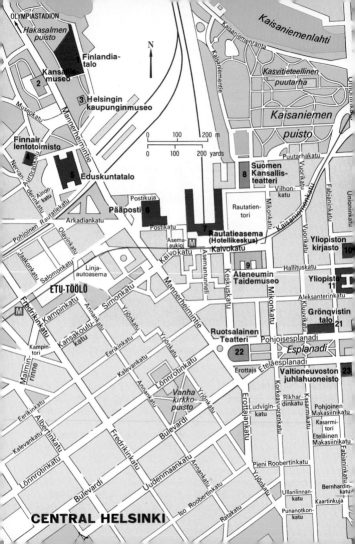

OLYMPIASTADION

Hakasalmen puisto

Finlandia-talo

Kansallis-museo **2**

3 Helsingin kaupunginmuseo

Finnair-lentotoimisto

5 Eduskuntatalo

Museokatu

Mannerheimintie

Nervan...

Arkadiankatu

Postikuja

Pääposti 6

Postikatu

Asemakatu

M

Kaivokatu

Linja-autoasema

ETU-TÖÖLÖ

Pohjoinen Rautatiekatu

Jaakonkatu

Salomonkatu

Olavinkatu

M

Fredrikinkatu

Kampinkatu

Simonkatu

Kansakoulu-katu

Annankatu

Yrjönkatu

Eerikinkatu

Kampin-tori

Kalevankatu

Malmin-rinne

Eerikinkatu

Albertinkatu

Kalevankatu

Lönnrotinkatu

Vanha kirkko-puisto

Annankatu

Bulevardi

Fredrikinkatu

Yrjönkatu

Uudenmaankatu

Annankatu

Iso Roobertinkatu

Ratakatu

Lönnrotinkatu

Bulevardi

Kaisaniemenlahti

Kaisaniemenranta

Kaisaniemenlahti

Kaisaniemenmäki

Kasvitieteellinen puutarha

Kaisaniemen puisto

Puutarhakatu

Suomen Kansallis-teatteri 8

Vilhon-katu

Mikonkatu

Vuorikatu

Rautatien-tori

7 Rautatieasema (Hotellikeskus)

Kaivokatu

Asematunneli

Keskuskatu

Hallituskatu

9 Ateneumin Taidemuseo

Mikonkatu

Aleksanterinkatu

Kluuvikatu

Ruotsalainen Teatteri

22

Pohjoisesplanadi

Esplanadi

Eteläesplanadi

Erottaja

Korkeavuorenkatu

Eteläesplanadi

Ludviginkatu

Erottajankatu

Kasarminkatu

Rikhar-dinkatu

Pieni Roobertinkatu

Yrjönkatu

Ullanlinnankatu

Punanotkon-katu

Kaisaniemenkatu

Fabianinkatu

Unioninkatu

Yliopiston kirjasto 10

Yliopisto 11

Grönqvistin talo 21

Valtioneuvoston juhlahuoneisto 23

Pohjoinen Makasiinikatu

Kasarmi-tori

Eteläinen Makasiinikatu

Fabianinkatu

Bernhardin-katu

Kaartinkuja

CENTRAL HELSINKI

0   100   200 m
0   100   200 yards

N

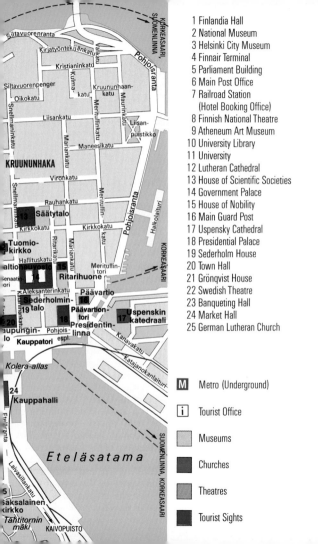

1 Finlandia Hall
2 National Museum
3 Helsinki City Museum
4 Finnair Terminal
5 Parliament Building
6 Main Post Office
7 Railroad Station
  (Hotel Booking Office)
8 Finnish National Theatre
9 Atheneum Art Museum
10 University Library
11 University
12 Lutheran Cathedral
13 House of Scientific Societies
14 Government Palace
15 House of Nobility
16 Main Guard Post
17 Uspensky Cathedral
18 Presidential Palace
19 Sederholm House
20 Town Hall
21 Grönqvist House
22 Swedish Theatre
23 Banqueting Hall
24 Market Hall
25 German Lutheran Church

M Metro (Underground)

i Tourist Office

   Museums

   Churches

   Theatres

   Tourist Sights

sphere seems to put everyone in a good mood. Shoppers gladly give directions to visitors, perhaps because a majority of the inhabitants of Helsinki were born elsewhere, and so were once strangers in the city themselves.

The tall neo-Classical obelisk that rises in the middle of the square is known as the **Czarina's Stone** (Keisarinnankivi). It commemorates the visit of the Czarina Alexandra to Helsinki in 1833, the first Russian empress to so honour the city. Local people are very fond of the monument, which they refer to as the "toothpick". Near the stone are a number of stalls selling souvenirs and crafts. Keep an eye out for slippery cobblestones as you stroll about.

Just off Market Square in a street called Eteläranta, a delightful Victorian indoor market, the **Kauppahalli,** has provided grateful townspeople with an alternative to outdoor shopping since 1888. Gratitude knows no bounds in winter, when even the Finns find the winds in Market Square rather brisk.

Now move on to Helsinki's handsome, neo-Classical **Town Hall** (Kaupungintalo), facing the market between Katariinankatu and Sofiankatu. This landmark dates from 1833 and was designed as a hotel by the tireless Carl Ludvig Engel, the architect responsible for so much of central Helsinki. The main hall is now the place for routine municipal council meetings, as well as occasional banquets and galas.

Two blocks east of the Town Hall, at the corner of Mariankatu, you'll see the dignified **Presidential Palace** (Presidentinlinna), where a stoical sentry usually stands guard. Only nominally a residence, the palace is used on state occasions.

The building dates from 1814 and was originally the home of a wealthy merchant. But when the town fathers decided Helsinki lacked an imperial residence, the house was purchased and turned over to the indispensable Engel, who remodelled it into a palace in 1843. Not until 12 years later did a czar, Nicholas I, actually stay there.

Walk around the corner to the Main Guard Post (Päävartio), a small blue building in its own square, protected by guardsmen in battle gear. The **Changing of the Guard** ceremony takes place here in summer, featuring a parade led through the centre of town by a band. While the display may be less lavish than that at Buckingham

Palace, enthusiastic spectators are no less delighted.

Cross the bridge over the canal connecting Eteläsatama (South Harbour) with Pohjoissatama (North Harbour) and you come to **Katajanokka,** a peninsula that was largely a shanty town of turf-roofed wooden buildings until late last century, despite proximity to the centre of the city. When development came, the prevailing architectural styles were the popular turn-of-the-century National Romanticism (see p. 41) and Art Nouveau, characterized by the use of organic forms.

The enormous red-brick Byzantine bulk of **Uspensky Cathedral** *(Uspenskin katedraali)* dominates Katajanokka. Perched on a steep hill overlooking South Harbour, the cathedral looms large on the Helsinki skyline, its central dome towering above the water. Uspensky, built in 1868 to serve Helsinki's Russian Orthodox community, is now the cathedral of the Finnish Orthodox Church, a small denomination. The cathedral is open long hours in summer, but in winter visits must coincide with services, which are chanted in sonorous Slavonic.

The cathedral's architects sought inspiration in the design of Constantinople's Hagia Sofia. The latter-day Finnish copy is spacious and richly decorated in red, blue and gold. There are, of course, many icons. Particularly noteworthy is the iconostasis, the screen in front of the high altar, on which hang Russian votive works dating from the time of the cathedral's founding.

South Harbour and Kaivopuisto

In fine weather, the short walk from Katajanokka to the Kaivopuisto district is a pleasant one. Stroll along South Harbour past docks busy with the loading and unloading of the modern ferries that shuttle to Sweden and Germany. Just offshore on the small island of Valkosaari you'll see a large fleet of pleasure boats moored alongside the oldest yacht club in Finland, founded in 1861.

Observatory Hill *(Tähtitorninmäki)* rises to the right at this point, and the **Astronomical Observatory** *(Tähtitorni)*, completed in 1833, crowns its 100-foot summit. The building, yet another major work by Engel, now belongs to Helsinki University. At the foot of the hill is the red brick German Lutheran Church *(Saksalainen kirkko)*, which dates from the

1860s, when there was a sizable German community.

Bear right on Laivasillankatu and walk up the hill. The trees of **Kaivopuisto** (Spa Park) will soon rise ahead. The park, which gives its name to the surrounding district, remains one of the most gracious of the city's green spaces, with delightful footpaths and splendid sea views.

The park was once part of a lively health resort developed in the 1830s and at the height of popularity in the middle decades of the 19th century, when the Russian nobility came by steamer from St. Petersburg just to take the waters. A tree-lined avenue leads to the former main spa building, originally designed by Engel in 1838, but much remodelled. The elegant setting created for the baths now lends its charm to a popular restaurant.

The Kaivopuisto district is famous for its ornate, Russian-style wooden **villas**—Slavic cousins of the 19th-century North American Carpenter's Gothic style. Most of the major embassies are to be found here, on or near Itäinen Puistotie.

There are also two interesting museums in the area, the Mannerheim Museum at Kalliolinnantie 14 and the Cygnaeus Art Collection at No. 8.

The century-old house that belonged to the Finnish soldier and statesman Carl Gustav Mannerheim has been opened to the public as the **Mannerheim-museo.** The bedroom, study, library and drawing room, preserved as they were in 1940, clearly express the marshal's soldierly taste for

Design shop overlooking Esplanadi
30 *shows off inventive wooden toys.*

simple comfort. You can see a collection of the great man's medals, uniforms, decorations and batons, along with mementoes of his journeys.

The **Cygnaeus Art Collection** *(Cygnaeuksen taidegalleria)* is housed in the wonderful turreted 1860s summer home of Fredrik Cygnaeus, a Helsinki University professor who was a leading figure in the mid-19th century national awakening and a friend of the most progressive artists of the day.

Forming the core of the collection, which includes both foreign and Finnish paintings, are works by such National Romantic artists as Walter Runeberg and Albert Edelfelt.

Esplanadi

Esplanadi (or "Espa", as it is popularly called) is an elegant boulevard that runs from Market Square to the beginning of Mannerheimintie, the city's main artery. It is divided by a park into two parallel

thoroughfares with slightly different characters, Pohjoisesplanadi (North Esplanade) and Eteläesplanadi (South Esplanade).

A plan for Esplanadi was approved as early as 1817, but construction proceeded slowly, with South Esplanade developing first, then North Esplanade in the 1880s. The latter traverses reclaimed land, which made building more difficult. Along Eteläesplanadi are banks, insurance and government offices and some shops. But the biggest and busiest shops line Pohjoisesplanadi, their stunning window displays featuring the best of Finnish design.

In the days when controversy raged as to whether Swedish or Finnish should be the official language, those favouring Swedish—which stood for official authority—promenaded on Pohjoisesplanadi, while the proponents of Finnish walked on the opposite side.

Both sides of the esplanade have their share of handsome, traditional buildings. One of the finest is the **Banqueting Hall of the Council of State** (*Valtioneuvoston juhlahuoneisto*) at the eastern end of Eteläesplanadi. This elegant little palace completed in 1824 was designed by Engel as a head-quarters for the Inspector-General of the Finnish Army. Later it was the residence of the Governor General of the Grand Duchy, and after that the Red Guard made it their administrative centre during the 1918 occupation of Helsinki. The building is still popularly called "Smolna", after Smolny Institute in Leningrad, Bolshevik headquarters in 1917. Now state functions are held here.

The ornate façade of **Grönqvist House** (*Grönqvistin talo*) extends along Pohjoisesplanadi from Fabianinkatu to Kluuvikatu. At the time of its completion in 1882, this was the largest private house in Finland.

Across from it on the western corner of Kluuvikatu you'll see a bank building in the same exuberant style. This is, in fact, a careful reproduction of the Hotel Kämp, which formerly occupied the site. Popular sentiment decreed that the new structure retain the appearance of the famous old establishment, frequented by Jean Sibelius, the composer, and others.

Be sure to stop for a beer or

32

Eliel Saarinen's design for railway station was years ahead of its time.

coffee at **Kappeli** (The Chapel), a convivial, charming and much-loved old restaurant and café opposite the Banqueting Hall at the eastern entrance to the park. It all began with a shepherd (known as *pastor*, Latin for "shepherd"), who sold milk from a stall on the site. By logical extension, his evolving establishment was christened "chapel". This is where the literati of the 19th century gathered, and the atmosphere of the period has been lovingly preserved.

Esplanade park offers a year-round display of statuary, in addition to temporary exhibitions of sculpture set up during the Helsinki Summer Festival. In the middle of the park stands Walter Runeberg's tribute (1885) to his father, Johan Ludvig, who achieved fame as the author of *Maamme* (Our Land), the Finnish national anthem. There are also likenesses of Zacharias Topelius, author of historical novels and well-loved fairy tales, and of Eino Leino, the greatest Finnish poet.

The horseshoe-shaped **Swedish Theatre** *(Ruotsalainen teatteri)*, the oldest Swedish-language theatre in bilingual Finland, anchors the western end of the park just as Kappeli holds down the eastern end.

Aleksanterinkatu

The Helsinki version of Fifth Avenue and Oxford Street runs parallel to Pohjoisesplanadi. Famed in Finland as the "Christmas Street", Aleksanterinkatu lights up annually with lavish decorations. The street forms the southern boundary of Senaatintori (see next page), and is named after Czar Alexander II.

The busiest corner is undoubtedly the crossroad with Mannerheimintie, for this is the site of Stockmann's, the largest department store in Finland. The statue of the *Three Smiths* outside makes a rendezvous for shoppers.

An underground passageway leads north from Aleksanterinkatu to the **City Centre,** a modern complex of shops and restaurants that attracts attention as much for its architecture as for the goods on sale. An underground tunnel lined with still more shops links the centre to the **Railway Station** *(Rautatieasema).* It is reminiscent of an enormous 1930s radio set, and its Art Deco style was nothing less than innovative in 1916, the year of its completion. The building figures among the masterworks of architect Eliel Saarinen, who won a competition for its design at the turn of the century.

East of the station, Rautatientori (Railway Square), an unsightly bog until the mid-19th century, pulsates with activity. Finland's fast, efficient rail and bus network makes the station and square (site of the city bus terminal) a popular place with commuters. Walk south-west of the square to the **Amos Anderson Art Museum** *(Amos Andersonin taidemuseo)* in Yrjönkatu. On view are canvases by the best of Finland's 20th-century painters: the cubist Marcus Collin, Eero Nelimarkka (noted for scenes of peasant life) and Helena Schjerbeck, an expressionist. A selection of more recent work can also be seen. North of Rautatientori looms the grey granite bulk of the **Finnish National Theatre** *(Kansallisteatteri)*, unequalled since 1872 for its Finnish-language productions. In front of the main entrance is an impressive statue by Wäinö Aaltonen, whose renown is equal to that of his subject—Aleksis Kivi, the great author and dramatist. Kivi's brilliant novel *Seven Brothers* transformed Finnish literature when it appeared in 1870.

Kaisaniemi sprawls to the north of the National Theatre building and alongside the railway yard. In the park, you'll find the Botanical Gardens *(Kasvitieteellinen puutarha)*, the country's largest botanical collection, and a greenhouse devoted to tropical plants.

Neo-Classical Sights

Senaatintori (Senate Square) lies at the heart of Ehrenström's concept of Helsinki. This masterpiece of early 19th-century city planning impresses without intimidating. Notice how perfectly one building balances another, creating an architectural entity that is among the most beautifully proportioned in Europe.

The most imposing of Senaatintori monuments, the **Lutheran Cathedral** *(Tuomiokirkko)*, was intended by architect Engel to be uncompromisingly neo-Classical, with one great dome. But on his death in 1840, another Prussian émigré, Ernst Lohrmann, took over the project. Fearing that a single cupola might not be sufficiently monumental, he added four smaller domes spangled with gilded stars, and lined the roof with copies of statues by Thorvaldsen in Copenhagen's Church of Our Lady. The result is striking, but not at all what Engel envisaged.

The main entrance to the cathedral faces Unioninkatu, though most visitors and worshippers approach from Senate

Square walking up the granite steps. In deference to both classical and Lutheran traditions, the interior is relatively simple and severe. There are statues of Martin Luther, Mikael Agricola (the great reformer who translated the New Testament into Finnish) and Philip Melanchthon, Luther's assistant and the interpreter of his teachings.

The most memorable ceremony to take place here was the funeral of Carl Gustav Mannerheim in 1951. His body lay in state in the cathedral for three days. The nation mourned and Senate Square was filled with Finns from every walk of life come to pay their last respects to the "Knight of Europe", as he was fondly known.

Government Palace *(Valtioneuvosto),* known before independence as Senate House, frames the east side of the square. The Imperial Senate sat here from 1822 onwards, having moved to Helsinki from Turku in 1819. The original Engel building has been much enlarged over the years and now occupies an entire street.

The main building of the **University** *(Yliopisto)* features Ionic columns, in contrast to the Corinthian order of the palace opposite. Some 22,000 students, equally divided into men and women, attend classes in both Finnish and Swedish. The institution is the country's only bilingual university. There is no centralized university campus, and classrooms are scattered around the city. Most of them are situated in the Kruununhaka (Pasture) district of Helsinki, so called because it was once crown pasturage.

Across from the west entrance to the cathedral stands the superbly graceful buff and white **University Library** *(Yliopiston kirjasto),* generally considered the finest of all Engel buildings. The library's excellent collection of books includes the most complete set of 19th-century Russian works in Western Europe. Access is restricted to students, scholars and researchers, but the public is allowed to go as far as the entrance hall.

The oldest stone structure in Helsinki (1757), **Sederholm House** *(Sederholmin talo),* contrasts with the neo-Classical splendour of the other buildings on the square. It is situated to one side at the corner of Aleksanterinkatu and Katarii-

Solemn state occasions take place in Helsinki's neo-Classic cathedral.

Helsinki's Mannerheimintie runs for three busy, distinguished miles.

nankatu. Had Sweden won the Great Northern War in 1721, instead of losing it to Russia, chances are this part of the city would be filled with houses designed along the same solid but unpretentious lines.

For some buildings in the vicinity of Senate Square, modern times have meant a change in status, if not dignity. The Finnish Diet convened in the ornate neo-Renaissance rooms of the **Säätytalo** (House of Scientific Societies) on Snellmaninkatu, renovated to accommodate state banquets and government functions. And noble families socialized at the neo-Gothic **Ritarihuone** (House of Nobility) in the small park off Aleksanterinkatu at Mariankatu, now a venue for concerts and exhibitions. Splendid coats of arms decorate the main hall, where de-

sentative government, and he personally attended the opening of the Diet in 1863. In fact, his statue has come to symbolize Finnish identity, and many nationalist demonstrations have been held in its shadow.

Mannerheimintie

Mannerheimintie, the longest street in Helsinki, begins at the western end of Eteläesplanadi and runs north-west for 3 majestic miles. The sweeping thoroughfare was renamed in honour of the marshal on his 75th birthday in 1942. A larger-than-life equestrian statue of the great soldier and statesman, shown in the fur cap he wore during his great victories in the Winter War, ornaments the avenue. It faces the Main Post Office *(Pääposti)*, a functional-looking yellow-brick cube.

scendants of the original families still gather from time to time.

It is fitting that a **statue** of Czar Alexander II stands at the centre of the architectural ensemble surrounding Senate Square. Alexander was a good friend to Finland, instituting reforms such as the recognition of Finnish as an official language and the creation of a separate monetary system. The czar was also responsible for the re-establishment of repre-

The political life of Finland centres around the grey granite **Parliament Building** *(Eduskuntatalo)*, a short distance from the Post Office. This solemn structure was completed in 1931. The one-chamber Parliament of 200 members (over 25 per cent of them women) is elected by proportional representation. Members meet in a domed chamber decorated with sculpture by Wäinö Aaltonen. Note that Parliament is **39** open to the public only when members are not in session.

From the Parliament Building, make a short detour into Töölö, the residential district that lies to the west of Mannerheimintie, to see the **Rock Church** *(Temppeliaukion kirkko)*, a spectacular example of modern Finnish ecclesiastical architecture designed by two brothers, Timo and Tuomo Suomalainen. They took as their starting point a rocky outcrop that rises some 40 feet (12 metres) above street level.

Acoustical excellence and unique design enhance the Rock Church.

The result is an ingenious modern version of the rotunda, with interior walls blasted from bedrock and spanned by a huge dome covered with copper wire. The plan was conceived from the inside out to achieve the maximum interior effect.

Since completion in 1969, the church has become one of the most frequented in Helsinki. In summer, English-language services are held for visitors. The Rock Church is also in great demand as a concert hall, thanks to excellent acoustics.

Now make your way back to Mannerheimintie and the

National Museum (*Kansallismuseo*), a local landmark standing in its own little park. This exuberant example of the National Romantic style was designed in 1902 by three distinguished architects: Armas Lindgren, Herman Gesellius and Eliel Saarinen. To express the national spirit, they incorporated features from historic Finnish buildings: the tower is reminiscent of the cathedral in Turku, the wall along Mannerheimintie resembles the ramparts of Vyborg Castle and there is a turret modelled after those of Olavinlinna, the famous fortress at Savonlinna. Native building materials were used throughout.

Visitors to the museum first have to go by a rather mournful stone bear, who stands guard outside the main entrance. You then pass through an ornamental bronze door into the entrance hall, decorated with frescoes by Akseli Gallen-Kallela illustrating the *Kalevala*, Finland's national epic. The work was designed for the Paris World Fair in 1900 and later repainted here.

The museum is a treasure-house of all things Finnish from prehistoric times to the present: You can see the remains of what is claimed to be the world's oldest fishing net, found in Karelia and dated to 6500 B.C., and inspect the throne used by Czar Alexander I at the Diet of Porvoo in 1809. There are pieces of medieval woodcarving and ingenious examples of peasant whittling.

Folk costumes from every part of the country are on display, along with splendid exhibits of traditional crafts. The hand-worked *ryijy* (pronounced rew-yew) rugs steal the show. One of the most colourful sections is that devoted to the lifestyles of the Estonians, Karelians, Livonians and other related peoples, not forgetting the most picturesque of all Finnish citizens—the Lapps.

Across from the National Museum, the **Helsinki City Museum** (*Helsingin kaupunginmuseo*) occupies a lovely neo-Classical mansion by Lohrmann, Villa Hakasalmi. The exhibits trace Helsinki's history from its founding to the present day and include a watercolour by Engel of Senate Square and a fascinating model of the city as it looked in 1870.

Next to Villa Hakasalmi rises that famed marble edifice, **Finlandia Hall** (*Finlandia-talo*), one of Europe's finest congress centres, incorporating a concert hall and restaurant. The complex comprises a main building (1971) and congress wing (1975), both designed by Alvar Aalto, whose bust is displayed in the grand foyer. Completed shortly before the architect's death in 1976, Finlandia Hall is not only Aalto's last major work, but also his masterpiece.

Guided tours of the complex are available; the schedule is irregular, depending upon the calendar of events. Enquire at the box office.

Hesperia Park

The park *(Hesperian puisto)* runs north of Finlandia Hall along the western shore of Töölönlahti. The amenities include a small summer restaurant, pedalos for hire and an ornamental jet of water. Across the bay from the Finlandia complex, you'll see the more austere but equally innovative **City Theatre** *(Kaupungin-teatteri)* by Timo Penttilä, which boasts a stage excavated from rock.

Follow the extension of Hesperia Park that runs west along Hesperiankatu to **Hietaniemi Cemetery** *(Hietaniemen hautausmaa),* established 150 years ago. Many of the great men of Finland are buried in the beautifully landscaped grounds, not least among them Carl Ludvig Engel. The grave of the Finnish Unknown Soldier is here, not far from that of his commander-in-chief, Carl Gustav Mannerheim. The marshal was laid to rest alongside more than 3,000 of his troops, fallen in battle during the Winter War. At Christmas lighted candles are placed on the graves in a moving gesture of tribute.

From the cemetery, it is a pleasant walk north along the water to **Sibelius Park** *(Sibeliuksen puisto)* a park laid out in honour of the composer

Child romps near the likeness of Sibelius, Finland's great composer; boat takes tourists to holiday isle.

Jean Sibelius. The lovely and largely natural grounds, broken up by rocky outcrops and shaded by old birch trees, preserve the kind of rugged Finnish beauty that inspired Sibelius in his work. To one side of the park stands a massive sculpture, the **Sibelius Monument,** created by Eila Hiltunen and dedicated to the musical vision of Sibelius. The work, unveiled in 1967 on the tenth anniversary of the composer's death, took six years to complete. Next to it is a relief of Sibelius, showing him as he looked at the height of his powers.

Helsinki's **Olympic Stadium** is situated to the east of Sibelius Park in another setting of greenery. It was constructed for the 1940 Olympic Games, which were cancelled when war broke out. Finland eventually hosted the games in 1952, a proud event that demonstrated the nation's remarkable post-war recovery to the world.

A stadium annex contains the **Sports Museum** (Urheilumuseo), with a library of 20,000 books on sports. The Olympic Games and highlights of Finnish sports history are the subject of displays. Of particular interest are the collection of antique skis and the mementoes of Paavo Nurmi, the "Flying Finn". Outside the stadium, a **statue** by Wäinö Aaltonen shows the great runner in full stride.

Climb to the top of the stadium **tower** (closed during games) for a marvellous panoramic view of Helsinki, then continue east until you see a large ferris wheel, the cheerful symbol of **Linnanmäki Amusement Park** (Linnanmäen huvipuisto). This permanent funfair offers thrilling rides on a roller coaster and carousel, as well as variety theatre performances and restaurants.

The Tourist Islands

This popular name for Helsinki's recreational archipelago is something of a misnomer, since local residents are the islands' most numerous and enthusiastic visitors. But there are facilities and space enough for everyone, and the islands certainly rank among the city's greatest tourist attractions. Convenient ferry and water-taxi services link the four main islands—Korkeasaari, Suomenlinna, Pihlajasaari and Seurasaari—to various points in central Helsinki. Korkeasaari and Seurasaari are also accessible by bridge.

Korkeasaari, site of the city zoo, has been the pride of Hel-

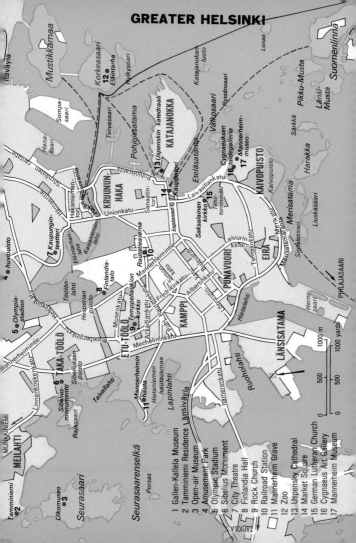

GREATER HELSINKI

1 Gallen-Kallela Museum
2 Tamminiemi Residence
3 Open-air Museum
4 Amusement Park
5 Olympic Stadium
6 Sibelius Monument
7 City Theatre
8 Finlandia Hall
9 Rock Church
10 Railroad Station
11 Market Square
12 Zoo
13 Uspensky Cathedral
14 Market Square
15 German Lutheran Church
16 Cygnaeus Art Gallery
17 Mannerheim Museum

Mustikkamaa
Itäväylä
Korkeasaari
12 ● Eläintarha
Hylkysaari
Sompa saari
Mustikkamaa
Hana saari
Tervasaari
Pohjoisatama
Katajanokan luoto
Lonaa
Suomenlinna
Pikku-Musta
Länsi-Musta
Vähäsaari
KATAJANOKKA
13 ● Uspenskin katedraali
Russänsaari
Särkkä
Harakka
Kruunun Haka
Siltavuorenranta
Hakaniemen Tori
Hakaniemenranta
Pohjoisranta
14 Kauppatori
Cygnaeuksen taidegalleria
16 ●
17 ● Mannerheim-museo
Kaivopuisto
Kaivopuisto
Eläintarhan lahti
Kaisaniemen lahti
Unionkatu
Senaatintori
Laivasillankatu
5 Tähti tornimäki
Liuskasaari
7 ● Kaupungin-teatteri
Kaisaniemenranta
Saksalainen kirkko
Esplanadi
Merisatama
Merikatu
Merisataman ranta
4 ● huvipuisto
Eläintarhan lahti
Töölön lahti
9 ● Finlandia-talo
Mannerheimintie
Ratakatu
Laivurin katu
EIRA
Siltasaarenkatu
Helsinginkatu
Hesperian puisto
Museokatu
Tempeliaukion kirkko
10 Rautatieasema
Simon
Fredrikinkatu
Albertinkatu
PUNAVUORI
Hietalahti
Sirpalesaari
5 ● Olympia-stadion
TAKA-TÖÖLÖ
6 ● Sibelius-monumentti
Sibeliuksen puisto
Töölön lahti
ETU-TÖÖLÖ
Mechelininkatu
Arkadiankatu
KAMPPI
Ruoholahti
Tämmerkatu
LÄNSISATAMA
Hernesaari
Mannerheimintie
1 ● hauta
Hietaniemen hautausmaa
Lapinlahti
Taivallahti
1000 m
500
1000 yards
0
500
MUNKKINIEMI
MEILAHTI
Tamminiemi
2 ●
Ulkomuseo
3 ●
Rajasaari
Seurasaari
Seurasaarenselkä
Porsas
Pihlajasaari

sinki since 1888. Considering the climatic limitations in what is said to be the world's northernmost **zoo,** the collection is remarkably varied and wide-ranging. More than a thousand animals are kept, including rare snow leopards and Siberian tigers and exotic specimens like the Australian wallaby and North American opossum. Many different kinds of birds can also be seen.

Even if there were no animals, Korkeasaari would still be worth visiting for its beaches and harbour views. It is an ideal place for a picnic, or for refreshment in one of several cafés and kiosks.

The trip to Korkeasaari takes about 10 minutes. Boats leave from Market Square *(Kauppatori)* every half hour in summer. There is also motorboat service from Hakaniemen ranta in the northeastern part of the city. In winter, Korkeasaari can only be reached by toll bridge via Mustikkamaa, another island.

Suomenlinna (Fortress of Finland), once known as the "Gibraltar of the North", is now no more than a recreational adjunct to Helsinki. But for nearly a century, the island group with its great fortress was an important community, and the tiny town of Helsinki

was the place where the garrison went for rest and relaxation.

The fortress was begun by the Swedes in 1748, and for a good part of its history was called Sveaborg (Fortress of Sweden). It was built in an attempt to contain Russian expansion into the Baltic, an objective enthusiastically endorsed by France. In fact, the French underwrote the cost of construction and undertook the building of the fleet that was based here.

The five main islands of Suomenlinna are inter-connected, so it is easy to stroll about. The ramparts make a popular promenade, and picnickers and sunbathers enjoy the artificial sand dunes created by the Russians in 1809 with sand imported from Estonia in an attempt to strengthen the defences.

An entire day can be spent exploring the old fortifications with their decorative cannon and attractive gardens. The architecture includes fine examples of various Swedish, French, Russian and Finnish styles. There is a popular bathing beach as well as several interesting museums. Small cafés and kiosks and a delightful restaurant add to the charm. Ferries leave from

Kauppatori every hour on the half hour. The **views** of Helsinki alone are worth the trip out.

The **Ehrensvärd Museum,** formerly the house of the commandant, is devoted to exhibits related to the remarkable Field Marshal (also Admiral) Augustin Ehrensvärd, who supervised construction of the fortress. Ehrensvärd was a scholar as well as a soldier, and it was his vigorous encouragement of the arts that made Suomenlinna such an important cultural centre. In addition to the personal belongings of Ehrensvärd, the museum displays a model of the fortress (useful for orientating yourself) and old maps, weapons and uniforms.

Not far away, Ehrensvärd lies buried in the ornate, Grecian-style sarcophagus that stands in the middle of the castle's lovely courtyard.

The **Armfelt Museum** occupies an 18th-century bastion, which provides the perfect setting for a collection of furniture and porcelain from the same period. The objects on show were taken from a manor house belonging to the distinguished Armfelt family.

The **Coastal Defence Museum** *(Rannikkotykistömuseo)* has found a fitting home in an old powder magazine. This branch of Helsinki's Military Museum devotes itself to the devices used to defend Finland's coast during the past 300 years. By far the most popular exhibit is the old coastal submarine *Vesikko,* tied up at Tykistölahti (Artillery Bay).

Pihlajasaari (Rowan Islands) comprises two small wooded islets connected by a footbridge. The little islands boast the best beaches for swimming and sunbathing in the Helsinki area, and the woods invite long walks and leisurely picnics. For the convenience of city-dwellers on fresh-air outings, a kiosk, café and changing huts have been provided. Daily motorboat service in summer links the island group to Merisatamaranta, a harbour west of Kaivopuisto.

Seurasaari accommodates both a national park with a bathing beach and recreation area and Finland's oldest and largest open-air museum *(Ulkomuseo).* The museum, founded in 1909, has inspired many similar installations.

Scattered about a setting of great natural beauty are more than 80 buildings gathered from all over Finland. They range from smoke-darkened peasant huts of a pattern unchanged since the Middle Ages to a 17th-century wooden **47** church from Karuna, still used for church services on Sunday. There are also some interesting examples of Lapp housing, including structures that resemble the North American Indian's teepee and granaries on log stilts identical to those used in Alaska and northern Canada.

Craft demonstrations, from weaving and wood-carving to threshing and tanning, are held throughout the summer, and the air is almost always filled with the sounds of folk music

Folk dancers perform in open-air museum amid rebuilt old houses.

and dancing. Seurasaari's **Festival Field** *(juhlakenttä)* is the site of folk festivals and competitions, and from mid-May to mid-October you may be lucky enough to see a rough and tumble Karelian game called *kyykkä.*

There is a restaurant and café on the museum grounds, and guided tours in English are available. Motorboats connect Kauppatori to Seurasaari, and a bus stops by the footbridge leading to the folk park.

Not far from Seurasaari's footbridge is Tamminiemi, the handsome villa where the president of Finland lives.

Day Trips

Gallen-Kallela Museum. West of Helsinki, just beyond the city limits on the outskirts of Espoo, lies the former home and studio of the painter Akseli Gallen-Kallela (1865–1931). He called the turreted house (completed in 1913) Tarvaspää after the peninsula on which it stands, and its rough, hand-plastered walls, rustic log floors and peasant-style furniture have been preserved as he left them.

Gallen-Kallela's brushes and personal effects fill the rooms, along with hundreds of examples of his work, ranging from early realism to something like modern symbolism. You can also view the painter's large and highly personal collection of ethnic art.

Espoo. Advanced architecture and a sophisticated city plan have won international recognition for the new town of Espoo. This model of modern urban design comprises several centres of habitation, including Tapiola Garden City and Otaniemi Institute of Technology.

Since receiving its charter in 1972, Espoo has become Finland's fourth-largest city, with a population of 150,000. Such rapid growth is due in large part to the migration of considerable numbers of the rural population to towns in the south. But the great beauty of Espoo's extensive field and forest setting and its modern and well designed town plan cannot be underestimated as contributory factors.

In 1951 a variety of citizens' groups founded **Tapiola.** The garden city occupies a vast site, spacious enough for 16,000 residents from all walks of life. Visionary planners like Alvar Aalto have provided a wide range of housing, from moderately priced multi-storey condominium complexes to expensive single-family bungalows. Disturbance of the environment has been kept to a minimum, and trees, gardens and foliage are everywhere in evidence.

A ring of greenery separates residential areas from the business district, a pedestrian island where motor traffic is banned. There are shops, restaurants, office towers, factories, an open-air market and a hotel. So many tourists come to marvel at this architectural *tour de force* that a tourist information office has been opened near the hotel.

Another Espoo centre, **Otaniemi**, is often called the "engineers' suburb", as it's the home of the Institute of Technology. A hotel, shopping centre, indoor sports stadium and tennis courts are available to the residents.

Alvar Aalto's hand can be discerned here, too. He was completely responsible for the design of the **Institute of Technology** *(Teknillinen korkeakoulu)*, completed in the 1960s and universally regarded as some of his best work. Take a look at the dramatic **Auditorium** with curving pitched roof—a modern, glassed-in northern version of the Greek amphitheatre. Equally striking is **Dipoli**, the Student Union building, a confection of native stone, wood and concrete designed by Raili and Reima Pietilä, a husband-and-wife team.

Many of the innovations carried out at Tapiola and Otaniemi have their origins in the work of Eliel Saarinen, Armas Lindgren and Herman Gesellius—the architects most responsible for creating the National Romantic style. There is no better illustration of their collective ingenuity than **Hvitträsk,** a fieldstone castle on Lake Vitträsk in Espoo. They designed the fanciful structure at the turn of the century to serve as a common studio and individual living quarters. Recent restoration has brought Hvitträsk back to its original state.

Frescoes by Gallen-Kallela can be seen, in addition to a display of Finnish handicrafts, some of which are for sale. The wooded park is very beautiful and the site was obviously selected for its inspirational qualities. The graves of Eliel Saarinen, his wife Loja and Herman Gesellius are at the foot of a large rock, shaded by ancient spruce trees.

Garden city of Tapiola fascinates town planners and tourists alike.

Ainola. The composer Jean Sibelius lived in a rural setting at Ainola, the house where he wrote five of his seven symphonies. "Here at Ainola the silence speaks", Sibelius said. The house is situated 39 kilometres north of Helsinki in the small town of JÄRVENPÄÄ. It was designed by Lars Sonck and named after the composer's wife Aino, who lived in the house from its completion in 1904 until her death in 1969 at the age of 97.

Only the ground floor is open to the public. The drawing room is dominated by the Steinway grand piano friends presented to Sibelius on his 50th birthday, and the walls are hung with paintings and mementoes. Sibelius' bedroom and study can be visited. Jean and Aino Sibelius are buried together in the garden, the graves marked by a simple slab of polished stone.

Aleksis Kivi Museum. The simple house in NURMIJÄRVI (some 20 km. directly west of Järvenpää) where the writer Aleksis Kivi grew up has been turned into a museum. Not only does the house present a picture of everyday life in 19th-century Finland, but it also provides us with glimpses of the boyhood of the "Mark Twain of Finnish literature".

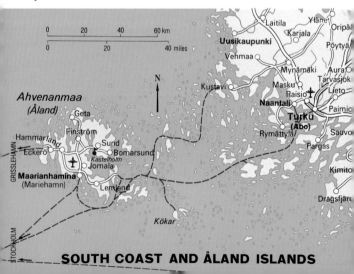

SOUTH COAST AND ÅLAND ISLANDS

South Coast

Centuries ago, Finland's beautiful, serrated southern coastline was the haunt of Vikings and the destination of pilgrims bound for its medieval shrines. Today yachtsmen and tourists appreciate the charms of the region.

Porvoo/Borgå

Picturesque Porvoo (50 km. east of Helsinki) is among the oldest and most historic of Finnish coastal towns. It was an important trading post years before its official founding in 1346 on a strategic site at the mouth of the River Porvoo.

The town was long a Swedish stronghold, and Swedish is still the mother tongue of nearly half its 20,000 citizens, who continue to call the place Borgå.

It isn't hard to see why Porvoo has always been a favourite of Finnish painters and poets. Streets lined with comfortably sagging wooden houses painted red, yellow and pale "Russian" blue meander through the old part of town by the river. The most photographed buildings are undoubtedly the bright red salt houses *(ranta-aitat)*, a row of eight 18th-century riverside warehouses. They stand in a

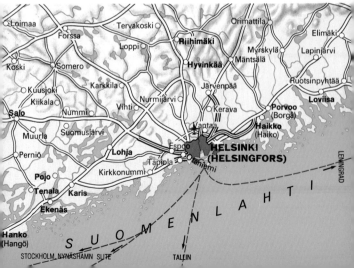

group, their colourful images reflected in the river. The warehouses survive unaltered, miraculously having escaped every one of the fires that ravaged the town.

The spire of the 15th-century **cathedral** (tuomiokirkko), a massive stone structure with walls six feet thick, rises over the old quarter. It was in Porvoo cathedral that Czar Alexander I opened the Diet in 1809 and declared the autonomy of the Grand Duchy of Finland—and himself its Grand Duke. The Runeberg statue of Alexander inside the cathedral portrays him as nothing less than a saint.

Near the cathedral in Museum Square (Museoaukio), an interesting local historical collection is on show at the Porvoo Museum. The **Edelfelt-Vallgren Museum** also faces directly on the square. Exhibits here outline the careers of sculptor Ville Vallgren, creator of Helsinki's *Havis Amanda*, and Albert Edelfelt, a leading painter of the turn of the century.

Porvoo's beloved native son, the national poet Johan Ludvig Runeberg, worked in the town

House of sculptor Ville Vallgren serves as museum in old Porvoo.

as a schoolteacher for more than 20 years. The wooden neo-Classical **Runeberg House,** another landmark of the old town, is open to visitors.

Nearby, the **W. Runeberg Gallery** presents sculpture created by the poet's son Walter. Not far away, in a small park beside the river, is a replica of Walter Runeberg's famous statue of his father in Helsinki's Esplanadi (see p. 34).

An old steamship graced with the name *J. L. Runeberg* sails daily from Helsinki to Porvoo, a distance of 31 miles. A stop is always made at HAIKKO, a neighbouring village with a beautiful and historic stately home, Haikko Manor, now converted into a luxury hotel and congress centre. The view from the terrace out over the Gulf of Finland is as spectacular now as it was when the Romanovs stopped here for tea in the days before the Russian Revolution.

Hanko/Hangö

This port town at the southern tip of Finland boasts a climate that is mild by Finnish standards, that is to say practically ice-free through the winter. Hanko (Hangö to the Swedish-speaking majority) was once the only port in Finland open to winter traffic, and an important naval base was situated here.

Late in the 19th century, Hanko emerged as a fashionable seaside spa, frequented by the Russian aristocracy. It remains a popular resort, and on summer week-ends the number of inhabitants (some 12,000) more than doubles. Special events like the famed Hanko regatta in mid-July attract hundreds of yachts. At this time of year, when the harbour is white with sails, no one disputes Hanko's claim to be the "yachting capital of Finland".

Holiday-makers are attracted by the town's superb beaches, with close to 9 miles of white sand, and the historic sights centered around **Itäsatama** (East Harbour). First and foremost is **Hauensuoli,** a group of rocks in the narrow strait of Tullisaari, accessible by waterbus from the harbour. From the 15th century on, passing sailors carved their names and coats of arms or trading emblems on the rocks, leaving a unique record of comings and goings.

To learn more about the history of the merchant marine, visit the Fortress Museum *(Linnoitusmuseo)* alongside the **55** harbour. In addition to the naval and military collections, there are exhibits recording local folk culture. You can also go up Hanko's tall concrete water tower, a navigational landmark. The observation deck offers bird's-eye views of beautiful coastal scenery.

Turku/Åbo

Finland's oldest city and its former capital, historic Turku is a pleasant riverside town and Baltic seaport of 165,000. The name means "market-place" in old Finnish, and it was as a trading settlement that Turku had its start before the 12th century.

Just about wherever you go here, you can see the spire of the medieval **cathedral** *(tuomiokirkko),* situated on a hill overlooking the River Aura. This became the seat of a bishop and the base from which the wild and pagan Finns were pacified and Christianized. The cathedral has been much enlarged and rebuilt over the centuries—even the famous spire dates from the 19th century. But its Gothic arches still soar majestically toward heaven and its thick walls defy time.

Tombs are not always tourist attractions, but Turku cathedral has some interesting ones. Several redoutable field marshals who fought with Sweden's King Gustavus Adolphus II in the Thirty Years' War were laid to rest here. Among them is the British mercenary Samuel Cockburn. English roses and Scottish thistles decorate his sarcophagus.

The most visited tomb is certainly that of Karin Månsdotter, who began her career as a flower girl in the local market and ended up as Queen of Sweden in 1568. The wife of Eric XIV, she is the only queen to be buried in Finland.

Also of interest are the medieval font of Finnish limestone, to the left of the main entrance, and the altar dedicated to Bishop Henry near the vestry. Long after the Reformation, Finns laid gifts to their former patron saint here. Carl Ludvig Engel designed the splendid pulpit of 1836.

Turku has long been an educational centre. Per Brahe founded Finland's first university here in 1640, but this institution was moved to Helsinki after the 1827 fire. Two universities now flourish in its place. Turku University *(Turun yliopisto)* serves the Finnish-speaking majority and Åbo Akademi, the minority

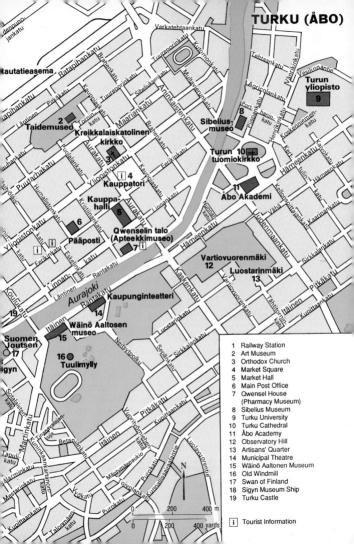

TURKU (ÅBO)

1 Railway Station
2 Art Museum
3 Orthodox Church
4 Market Square
5 Market Hall
6 Main Post Office
7 Qwensel House
  (Pharmacy Museum)
8 Sibelius Museum
9 Turku University
10 Turku Cathedral
11 Åbo Academy
12 Observatory Hill
13 Artisans' Quarter
14 Municipal Theatre
15 Wäinö Aaltonen Museum
16 Old Windmill
17 Swan of Finland
18 Sigyn Museum Ship
19 Turku Castle

[i] Tourist Information

Flowers everywhere: at market in Turku and on the river bank.

Swedish speakers. Both lie near the cathedral in the area known as the Old Great Market, scattered with fine neo-Classical buildings.

The Aura winds through the heart of Turku, and most of the important tourist sites are to be found on or near the river. The **Sibelius Museum,** north of the cathedral directly alongside the Aura, exhibits memorabilia relating to the career of composer Jean Sibelius. In addition, there is a fascinating display of musical instruments from around the world. Concerts of Sibelius programmes are sometimes given in the museum galleries.

The cathedral so monopolizes the ecclesiastical scene in Turku, that it is easy to forget there are other churches in the city. One of the most interesting is the **Orthodox Church** *(Kreikkalaiskatolinen kirkko),* across the Aura in Kauppatori (Market Square). The church bears a strong resemblance (on a smaller scale) to Helsinki's cathedral, and the architect was none other than Carl Ludvig Engel, ever-faithful to the neo-Classical style. However severe and formal the exterior may be, the church glows inside with golds and blues.

The cobbled expanse of Turku's colourful Market Square fronts the Orthodox Church. The time-honoured **Market Hall** *(Kauppahalli)* stands nearby.

Also in the neighbourhood, Turku's **Art Museum** *(Taidemuseo)* features Finnish painting and sculpture from the early 19th century to the present day.

Walk south of Kauppatori to the western bank of the Aura and you come to **Qwensel House** *(Qwenselin talo)*, the residence of a prosperous 18th-century merchant. This is Turku's oldest wooden building, and one of the few that survived the 1827 fire. The Pharmacy Museum *(Apteekkimuseo)* is housed within.

Turku's great fire was the biggest in Finnish history, destroying more than 2,500 buildings and virtually level-ling the old town. But the artisans' quarter, Luostarinmäki, survived intact, protected by the bulk of Vartiovuorenmäki (Observatory Hill). You may want to have a look at the Shipping and Navigation Museum in the old observatory. An interesting astronomical collection is also on display. But the main sight is Luostarinmäki itself, for the district forms the precincts of an open-air museum.

Awarded the Golden Apple **59**

prize (1984) for its contribution to tourism, **Luostarinmäki** is unique in Scandinavia. None of the 18 buildings in the museum area are reconstructions. They have been standing on the site since the 1700s, and for over two centuries have been put to use as artisans' workshops. Printers, potters, shoemakers, woodworkers and other traditional craftsmen have long plied their trades in Luostarinmäki.

The quarter is at its liveliest during Handicraft Days, an annual crafts fair held in late summer or early autumn. But even when a fair isn't in progress, Luostarinmäki's narrow dirt lanes, sagging wooden houses and tiny tree-shaded courtyards delight visitors. One popular stop is the Kisälli, a coffee house where hand-crafted articles are offered for sale.

The sleek **Wäinö Aaltonen Museum** makes a striking contrast to the quaint charm of Luostarinmäki. The museum stands downriver, next to the impressive Municipal Theatre *(Kaupunginteatteri)* and the Old Windmill *(Tuulimylly),* two Turku landmarks. On exhibit are works by Aaltonen (1894–1966), Finland's great 20th-century sculptor. Here you'll find the *Maid of Finland, Wading Girl* and *Head of Sibelius,* as well as a collection of the artist's comparatively little-known paintings. The museum includes work he did at the Turku Art Society School. After making the rounds of the galleries, rest awhile at the popular museum café, which looks out over the river.

On the same side of the river, you'll see two old sailing ships anchored side by side. One, the white-hulled *Suomen Joutsen* (Swan of Finland) was a naval cadet ship. It is closed to the public, but its neighbour, the three-masted bark **Sigyn,** has been converted into a floating museum. The *Sigyn,* christened in 1887, once sailed the world with cargoes of Finnish timber.

Turku Castle *(Turun linna)* rivals the cathedral as the city's great historic attraction. The castle (south-west of the centre) began life around 1280 as a fortified camp on an island at the mouth of the Aura. The gradual rising of the Finnish land mass has left the site high and dry, while centuries of building have turned the simple camp into an imposing structure.

A spacious and airy suite of **Renaissance rooms** was constructed on the top floor of the medieval castle in the 16th century by Duke John (later King John III of Sweden) and his wife, the Polish Princess Catherine Jagellonica. The splendour of their legendary court life ended abruptly in 1563

Wandering among 13th-century memories inside Turku Castle.

when John's brother, King Eric XIV of Sweden, besieged and occupied the castle, sending the fun-loving couple back to Sweden. (Seven years later, John captured Eric—and locked him up for a year.)

Like Turku's cathedral, the castle typifies Finnish nationhood. Care has been taken that it be a living symbol. The castle was badly bombed during World War II, and rebuilding it was a complicated job that took 15 years. Today the beautifully restored structure is used for concerts, civic banquets and meetings. Every year in August banquets organized for tourists recreate the aura of the castle's Renaissance heyday.

The castle contains the city's **Historical Museum** *(Historiallinen museo)*, featuring exhibitions of weapons, handicrafts and art, including some fine medieval woodcarvings.

Finland's south-western archipelago of islands, a favourite haunt of yachtsmen, extends as far as the Åland islands. **Ruissalo,** the most frequented of the islands, lies directly opposite Turku harbour, and a bridge connects it to the mainland. The island has been developed as a sports centre, with bathing beaches, a golf course and a campsite. **61**

Naantali

This old town, 16 kilometres west of Turku, grew up around the walls of a convent founded by the Swedish Order of St. Bridget in 1438. Today all that remains of the venerable religious centre is its sturdy stone church and its name, *Vallis Gratiae* (Valley of Grace).

St. Bridget's Church *(Pyhän Birgitan kirkko)* stands just above Naantali's busy little harbour. The parish church looks much as it did when the Bridgetine nuns filed in each day to sing the hours. The organ is a fine one, while the ornate pulpit has inscriptions in both Latin and Low German. Services now are Evangelical Lutheran, of course.

The surrounding district of medieval wooden buildings has survived unchanged since those long-ago days when pilgrim processions made their way through the winding streets. As you stroll about, poke your head into some of the handsome courtyards in the area. You'll discover that behind one worthy old building there is often another, even more ancient. The **Town Museum** *(Kaupunginmuseo)* stands in just such a courtyard. The collection comprises local artefacts and memorabilia.

Naantali has a long-standing reputation as a centre for crafts, particularly textiles. Many local handicrafts are a legacy of the Bridgetines—some of whom settled in the town when the Reformation ended the cloistered life.

After the convent was closed, the population fell below 700, and Naantali was the smallest chartered borough in Finland. But the town's fortunes revived in the 1800s with its development as a spa and a pioneer summer resort. Wander through the **spa park** and admire the Victorian charm of the surrounding buildings. During the spa's 19th-century heyday, enterprising townsfolk solved a housing shortage by taking up residence in their saunas and renting their houses to summer visitors. Now that Naantali has a population of more than 8,000, accommodation has improved. These days, the modern Naantali Health Spa offers visitors full spa treatment (see p. 117). Crowds converge on the town on July 27 for Sleepy Heads Day. Every year someone who has trouble struggling out of bed in the morning is elected *unikeko* (sleepy-head). Townspeople rudely awaken him at 6–7 a.m., dunk him in the sea, and a day of festivities begins.

Åland

Everywhere you look in Åland (pronounced O-land and called Ahvenanmaa in Finnish), you see islands, some 6,500 in fact —most of them tiny, almost all uninhabited. The archipelago forms an independent region within the frontiers of Finland that is officially recognized as belonging culturally to Sweden, just 30 miles away. The flag that flies in Åland is not the blue-and-white Finnish banner, but Åland's own, com-posed of a red and yellow cross on a blue field.

Through most of its history, Åland, like Finland, was a pos-session of Sweden, but it passed into Russian hands in 1809 and became part of the Grand Duchy of Finland. The Russians prized Åland for its strategic situation at the mouth of the Gulf of Bothnia, be-tween the gulf and the Baltic. With the Åland archipelago in Russian hands, the gulf was no longer a Swedish lake, but Ålanders continued to regard themselves as Swedes.

When Finland declared its independence after the Russian Revolution of 1917, Åland

Along with fishing, weaving is an old tradition of Åland archipelago.

sought return to Sweden. However, Finland proved reluctant to surrender strategic territory and Sweden, while understandably sympathetic, was not eager to go to war with Finland over the matter. So the "Åland Question" was referred to the League of Nations. The problem was resolved in 1921 by granting Finland sovereignty over the islands, but giving them autonomy and stipulating that the archipelago be demilitarized. There was some grumbling, but the agreement brought to Åland the tranquillity that tourists find so irresistible today.

Autonomy means that Ålanders have their own parliament or *Landsting*, which exercises full control over internal affairs. The official language is Swedish, and Åland men are exempt from Finnish military service—unlike their counterparts on the mainland. Åland has its own postage stamps, but when it comes to counting profits, the Ålanders do it in Finnish marks, the official currency. And there are considerable profits to count. The shipping and fishing industries are both thriving and more than two million tourists visit the islands annually, most of them Swedes from Grissle-

hamn, Kapellskär and Stockholm. A combination of scenic beauty and moderate prices (especially for alcohol purchased on board ship) attracts them to the islands.

Maarianhamina/ Mariehamn

The hub of tourist activity in Åland is the capital of Mariehamn on the island Ålanders call *fastlandet*, Swedish for "main land". The town of 10,000 is the largest of the 15 Åland communities and home to nearly half the inhabitants of the islands.

Mariehamn was founded in 1861 at the command of Czar Alexander II, who named it after his Czarina Maria. Even now the relaxed resort retains a certain imperial dignity. The town is quartered by two broad esplanades planted with handsome lindens, which earned Mariehamn the title of "Town of a Thousand Linden Trees". **Norra Esplanadgatan** (North Esplanade) runs the width of the town, a distance of more than half a mile, linking Mariehamn's two busy harbours. Across the central strip of park on Storgatan is the Ålands Museum, where exhibits illustrate different periods and aspects of Åland life.

Motorboats and yachts dock

at **East Harbour** *(Östra Hamnen)*, a small port dominated by the Self-Government House *(Självstyrelsehuset)*, where the islands' parliament meets. The building also serves as a congress and administrative centre.

Åland's far-ranging merchant navy, heir to a magnificent sea-faring tradition, bases itself at **West Harbour** *(Västra Hamnen)*. The thoroughly nautical atmosphere of the port is all you would expect from a shipping centre that ranks second after Helsinki. A statue entitled *Man at the Wheel* has been erected in the harbour as a memorial to sailors lost at sea, and adjacent to it stands the **Åland Maritime Museum** *(Ålands Sjöfartsmuseum)*.

This virtually unique collection of maritime objects pays tribute to the centuries-old shipping and sailing history of Åland, from the time of the Vikings to the days of the windjammers. On display are figureheads, seascapes, ships' models, sailors' gear, even small boats and entire windjammer cabins. Of all the exhibits in the museum the most impressive are those relating to the great Åland windjammer fleet, which continued to sail the seven seas well into the 1940s.

Tied up just a few yards from the museum is a magnificient surviving specimen of that fleet, the 310-foot-long, four-masted barque **Pommern.** Now a museum ship, the steel-hulled vessel is the very epitome of the Golden Age of Sailing. The *Pommern*, last of her class to be preserved in the original state, was built in Scotland for a German firm in 1903.

The proud ship was owned by the noted Åland shipping magnate, Captain Carl Gustav Erikson. She carried grain from Australia to England in her heyday, before World War II, twice winning the annual windjammer "Grain Race". The massively graceful *Pommern*, surrounded by small sailing yachts, looks rather like a whale amid a school of herring. Even with sails stowed, she inspires awe. The mainmast towers a dizzying 160 feet above the deck. Almost as impressive are the great cargo holds—dark, empty, echoing caverns into which nearly 50,000 bags of grain were packed.

Island Sights

Beyond Mariehamn stretches a lovely, unspoiled landscape of groves and meadows, ornamented with a dazzling vari- **65** ety of flowers, trees and shrubs. At **Ramsholmen,** a nature reserve 4 kilometres west of Mariehamn, you can find nearly 40 different kinds of plants within ten square feet. But you needn't be a botanist to appreciate the natural beauty around you.

The most popular main island excursions visit the ruined fortresses of Kastelholm and Bomarsund to the northeast of Mariehamn in the district of Sund.

Kastelholm was once the seat of Swedish power in Åland, and its halls knew the tread of the Swedish kings Gustavus Vasa, Gustavus Adolphus II and the luckless Eric XIV (who spent some time in the dungeon). The 14th-century castle, a partial ruin, was destroyed by fire in the 18th century. One wing has been re-built to accommodate the **Åland Historic Museum.** This eclectic and somewhat cluttered collection of Ålandiana, with particular emphasis on folk arts and crafts, nicely complements the official Ålands Museum in Mariehamn.

Be sure to visit the nearby open-air museum, the **Jan Karlsgården.** Old farm houses, barns, saunas and other typical Åland buildings conjure up an idyllic picture of rural life.

There are almost always musicians on hand to play the lively folk tunes that express so well the vitality of Åland.

The Russians began construction of **Bomarsund** in 1830, but the fortress was only half finished when the Crimean War broke out 23 years later. A combined Anglo-French force captured the fortification and systematically demolished the redoubts and ramparts. Bomarsund was never rebuilt. The rubble was quarried and all that remains now are picturesque piles of stones grown over with moss. There are six cemeteries near by, one for each of the major religious denominations represented in a garrison drawn from every corner of the Russian empire.

Åland is noted for its **medieval churches,** some dating from the 12th century, built of weathered, rough-hewn local stone. Their interiors are dark and cool, the white lime-washed walls brightened here and there by a colourful fresco that somehow survived the reformer's paint brush. A typical feature is the ship's models

Chequered history of Åland's Swedish-speaking people may be traced in stones of its churches.

suspended from the ceiling, gifts of grateful sailors whose prayers for rescue were answered.

Many of these churches are architectural gems in rural settings, beautifully sited overlooking the water. Some particularly fine ones are to be found at JOMALA, FINSTRÖM, HAMMARLAND, ECKERÖ, SUND and LEMLAND—all an easy drive (or a reasonable pedal) from Mariehamn.

In many villages on the main island, as elsewhere in Åland, you'll see colourful **maypoles,** regardless of the time of year. Look for tall tree trunks festooned with ribbons and wreaths, ship's models and weather vanes. Although used only once a year on Midsummer's Eve, the poles (a Swedish tradition) are left in place to the enhancement of the countryside.

Åland's 550 miles of road connect to an efficient ferry system that makes inter-island

travel not only possible, but practical. You can explore the gently rolling terrain by car or bicycle, or travel in the dependable and convenient coaches. If you decide to visit the more remote of Åland's thousands of islands and skerries, a hired boat becomes a necessity.

Åland sea, reflecting lazy clouds, is calm as a pond, but many island sailors have been lost in storms.

The Lake District

Finland is a land of water. No one knows exactly how many lakes there are, although the conveniently rounded figure of 62,000 is generally accepted. While lakes are found abundantly in almost every part of the country, water and land areas are about equal in the south-east.

The lakes are busy waterways, carrying both passengers and cargo—especially paper,

timber and other forest products. Transport ranges from barges and motor launches to hydrofoils and liners. Romantic old teak-trimmed steamers continue to ply many routes. Note that passenger services, excursion boats and cruise ships operate only from May to September.

Great Saimaa

The town of **Lappeenranta** serves as the gateway both to Great Saimaa *(Suur-Saimaa)* and the Soviet Union. The municipality that was founded by Queen Christina of Sweden in 1649 as a frontier fortress became a border town again at the end of World War II, and it shares a seven-mile boundary with the U.S.S.R.

From Lappeenranta begins the scenic route north through historic Karelia and Kainuu, two eastern provinces, known as the **"Bard and Border Way"**. It crosses the region where Finland's national epic, the *Kalevala*, was collected in the last century and parallels the eastern frontier.

Day trips by boat from Lappeenranta to VYBORG, just over the Soviet border, are so popular that bookings must be made at least two weeks in advance. You sail south-east through the Saimaan kanava, a canal inaugurated in 1856. Today, five of the eight locks are in Russian possession. From Vyborg connections can be made to Leningrad*. (No visas are required for the Vyborg leg of the journey.)

The canal is not as busy now as in the days when it was an all-Finnish route, but there is still considerable traffic. You'll see Russian barges carrying birch logs to Finland for sale. It seems rather like carrying coals to Newcastle, until you realize the Finns have established yearly cutting quotas to protect their own growing trees. After the 1968 re-opening of the canal, which had been closed since World War II, Lappeenranta flourished as a shipping centre.

The local economy also benefits from the presence of the giant Kaukas Pulp and Paper Mill, one of the largest in Northern Europe. In spite of the fact that its huffing and puffing befouls the air, there are few complaints from the population of 54,000. The plant employs most of the labour force, and workers speak of the odour as "the smell of money".

Military traditions are re-

---

* See the Berlitz travel guide to LENINGRAD for information on sightseeing in the city.

LAKE DISTRICT

spected in Lappeenranta and the town takes pride in the preservation of the citadel area (presently under restoration). A section of the fortress houses the South-Karelian Museum (Etelä-Karjalan maakuntamuseo), where displays tell the story of Viipuri, once Finland's second-largest city. Viipuri was incorporated in the U.S.S.R. as Vyborg after World War II. The Ratsuväki Museum, in an 18th-century guardhouse, traces the history of the Finnish cavalry from medieval times to the last years of World War II, when, according to one diorama, the once-terrifying Death's Head Hussaas were mounted

on bicycles. Also within the citadel is the oldest **Orthodox church** (Ortodoksinen kirkko) in Finland, built nearly 200 years ago.

The delightful lake resort of **Savonlinna** (north of Lappeenranta) makes a popular and convenient base for Lake District explorations. The "Pearl of the Saimaa" is one of the chief cities of eastern Finland's Savo province. Its story-book castle, Olavinlinna, epitomizes the romantic attractions of Fin-

Old-fashioned steamer chugs past peaceful lake district countryside.

land, and an opera festival is held each July in the castle courtyard.

Savonlinna sprawls across a series of islands. One of them, **Vääräsaari** (Spa Island) is the site of Finland's first casino and spa, built in the mid-1800s. Business boomed when the czar, hoping to solve his balance-of-payments problems by imposing currency restrictions, forbade the free-spending Russian aristocracy to visit Baden-Baden, Carlsbad and other foreign watering spots. There was a rush to Savonlinna. The baths are still in use, and they form part of a modern hotel complex. The old Victorian casino near by has been converted into a restaurant. A footbridge connects Vääräsaari to the city centre.

There are usually several picturesque old steamers tied up at the quay alongside Savonlinna's colourful Kauppatori (Market Square). One century-old lake steamer, the **Salama,** which foundered and sank in 1898 after 25 years of service on the St. Petersburg run, was hauled from the bottom and restored as a museum of lake traffic. Fascinating old photographs are exhibited, but the main attraction is the sturdy hull with its patched-up hole.

A footbridge from the main island crosses a tiny islet to **Olavinlinna,** the symbol of Savonlinna. The castle is surrounded by water, and a floating bridge spans its natural moat. Although frequently besieged during its 500 years of existence, Olavinlinna remains the best-preserved stone fortification in Finland.

The castle's double walls and three massive towers took 14 years to build—and just about the same length of time to restore. The work was completed in 1975 and included installation of a central heating system, a useful amenity overlooked by the founders. Left in place, however, is Northern Europe's oldest indoor lavatory, a cozy little stone affair which hangs over the moat.

The castle is used year-round for all sorts of plays, concerts, congresses and exhibitions. The opera festival was first held at Olavinlinna in 1912. After a long hiatus, performances were resumed in 1967 and have been held ever since. This major international event attracts artists of the first rank, and while it is in progress, Savonlinna is transformed from a slow-paced provincial resort into a glittering star of the European festival circuit.

The opera festival isn't the only summer musical event in Savonlinna. Concerts and recitals are given in an enormous **wooden church** situated at KERIMÄKI, a village 22 kilometres away. The huge structure was built in 1848, and its vast interior, with two-tiered balconies, holds a crowd of 3,000—more than half the village population.

The natural beauty of the Savonlinna region has inspired many Finnish writers and artists, especially the poet Johan Ludvig Runeberg, who composed some of his best work here. Particularly associated with the poet is **Punkaharju,** a ridge 5 miles long and as little as 25 feet wide formed during the Ice Age. It stretches between Pihlajavesi and Puruvesi just east of Savonlinna. A road and rail line run along it, offering splendid vistas.

A monument known as Runeberg's Knoll *(Runebergin kukkula)* has been erected at a hillock on the ridge in memory of the poet. The area is a great favourite of hikers and nature lovers, and there are two campsites and a holiday cottage colony.

Just beyond Savonlinna is **Rauhalinna,** a wooden extravaganza of a country house that has been converted into a hotel. This architectural fantasy, built in the last century by a Finnish general, combines Slavic, Biedermeier, Byzantine, Empire, even Maori elements. Just looking at it is ex-

The Sauna

An authentic Finnish sauna (the "au" is pronounced like the "ow" in "cow") is a small hut on a lakeshore, used every Saturday evening (more often in summer) for washing and relaxing. It is equipped with a wood-burning oven filled with stones, which are heated to bring the temperature up to between 80° and 100° C. Periodically, steam *(löyly)* is created, which raises the temperature even higher.

Bathers seat themselves on high, wooden benches *(lauteet)*, and gently whisk their bodies with bunches of birch twigs *(vasta* or *vihta)* to increase circulation. After the *löyly* bath, they plunge in the lake, then wash themselves in the sauna or an adjoining washroom. The procedure—heat, steam, lake—can be repeated several times.

Afterwards, you feel pleasantly relaxed, purified in body and soul. Finns regard the sauna as a national institution, from which no foreigner is allowed to escape, for his or her own benefit.

hausting. A 90-foot tower with a marvellous panoramic view over Lake Haapavesi rises out of a forest of gables.

Savonlinna is the terminus for a fleet of some 10 lake ships which sail regularly to Joensuu, Kuopio, Mikkeli, Lappeenranta and other Saimaa towns. Sights near and far are accessible by Saimaa excursion boats.

One of the most beautiful excursion routes from Savonlinna follows the eastern channel of Suur-Saimaa to Kuopio, chief port of the northern part of the lake chain. This is known as the Heinävesi route, named after the pretty town that straddles its narrowest point. Cruising along it, you'll be struck by the number of lakeside summer houses— every one with its own sauna.

After their steamy sauna sojourn, a Finnish family takes a dip in invigoratingly cold water of lake.

Finns own more week-end cottages than they do automobiles, and there are approximately one million saunas—or one for nearly every five Finns. Most of them are huts on lakes like this. Finnish lakes are very shallow, however, and to prevent pollution (and preserve the scenic beauty), home construction right on the lake shore is restricted these days.

HEINÄVESI is the home of **Uusi Valamo,** an Orthodox monastery transferred at the

Russian influence on history of Finland seen in church and icons.

end of World War II from an island in Lake Ladoga, now part of the Soviet Union. The beautiful new Byzantine-style church is decorated with a fine collection of icons, removed from the old monastery.

Some 20 kilometres away at LINTULA, a small Orthodox convent bears witness to the vitality of Eastern Christianity

in this part of Finland. The nuns keep bees and make beeswax candles.

Journey's end comes at **Kuopio,** a bustling town of 75,000 inhabitants that is every bit a daughter of the lake country. Activity centres on **Kauppatori** (Market Square) and the adjacent Market Hall *(Kauppahalli),* a good example of Art Nouveau architecture. People come from all over Savo to buy and sell in the market, one of the largest and liveliest in a region where people are noted for their warmth and humour.

The stalls that attract the thickest crowds are those selling *kalakukko,* a loaf of rye bread into which pork and the local white fish have been baked. *Kalakukko* is Kuopio's particular speciality, but you can also sample *karjalanpiirakka* (Karelian pie) and other delicacies associated with the region of Karelia, most of which was lost to Russia in World War II.

Many Karelians settled in Kuopio and the surrounding Savo region after the war, bringing with them a rich folk tradition and the Orthodox faith. Kuopio is now the seat of the Finnish Orthodox Church to which about 75,000 Finns belong. The head of the church, the Orthodox archbishop, resides in a modern complex that includes a seminary for the training of priests and the highly interesting **Orthodox Church Museum** *(Ortodok-sinen kirkkomuseo)*, a treasure house of priceless and beautiful works of religious art.

On display are some 2,000 objects drawn from the great monasteries of Valamo, Konevitsa, and Petsamo, as well as several Karelian parishes. The fleeing faithful were forced to abandon all but the finest icons, vestments and altar fixtures. Only the best of these are on view in Kuopio: a thousand-year-old jewelled cross, silver cenotaphs which once

held relics of saints, "Holy Doors" painted to illustrate the gospels.

Rare artefacts include special iron chains worn by penitent hermits and enormous, gold-covered, jewel-encrusted Bibles. And then, of course, there are the icons. Rich and glowing examples of different schools and centuries are represented, all of them superb. To visit the Orthodox Museum is to absorb an entire culture, and leave enriched.

Savo's own vital folk culture takes first place at the **Kuopio Museum,** and the building itself is another fine example of Art Nouveau. The attractively exhibited examples of peasant arts and crafts range from ingenious tools and weapons to beautiful weavings and woodcarvings. The most unusual displays relate to the working of birch bark, a local speciality. Not only are there attractive mats and baskets made of bark strips, but even clothes and boots *(virsut).* Another section of the museum presents natural history and historical exhibits, including displays of Stone Age implements found in the area.

Crafts remain a vital part of Finnish life as can be seen at the **Kotiteollisuusopisto** (Institute of Handicraft), a school for artisans and craftsmen on Piispankatu. A shop sells textile, ceramic, wood and metal products made by gifted students, and the institute operates an attractive little restaurant open daily.

Wherever you are in Kuopio, you can see the city's most

From 225-foot observation tower of Kuopio, view is 360 degrees of trees, islands and cool lakes. **79**

prominent feature, the 225-foot **observation tower** that rises high above a hill called Puijo, 2 kilometres north of the city centre. The tower has become one of Finland's most popular tourist attractions, famed for the views across Lake Kallavesi, almost 675 feet below. Take the lift to the panorama platform, or better still enjoy a meal in the tower's revolving restaurant and let the view come to you.

In all directions, lakes and islands stretch away to the horizon in a mosaic of greens and blues. There is an old Finnish fairy tale about a lake in which there was an island, in which there was a lake, in which there was an island, in which there was a lake ... The storyteller responsible for the tale must have climbed to the top of Puijo.

In winter, major sports competitions, including international slalom, downhill racing and ski jumping, are held at Puijo. Near the base of the tower is a ski lodge dating from 1903, still a popular resort.

Kuopio's lively appreciation of the performing arts comes to the fore in the Dance and Music Festival held each June. Most of the events take place outdoors in the market-place, where the cultural and the commercial, the artistic and the agricultural all come together in one joyful celebration.

Central and Western Lakeland

There are, of course, major lake regions besides Suur-Saimaa. The city of **Lahti,** built on the shores of Lake Vesijärvi (which is in turn an arm of Lake Päijänne), marks the south-central limits of the Lake District. Although there is some tourist activity in summer, Finland's sixth-largest city is better known as a winter resort and the host of the Finlandia Ski Race in February, a major cross-country event.

The westernmost route through Lakeland crosses a beautiful stretch of country, connecting the old town of HÄMEENLINNA (with a 13th-century castle and the house in which Sibelius was born) in the south-west to **Tampere,** one of Finland's most important industrial towns and a leading textile-manufacturing centre. Tampere's population of 170,000 makes it the second-largest city in Finland. Because of its importance as a textile centre, Tampere is called the "Manchester of Finland", but the city actually bears little resemblance to the British city.

Thanks to a waterfront situation near the rapids that run between lakes Näsijärvi and Pyhäjärvi, Tampere is about as attractive as you could reasonably expect an industrial community to be. There are, for instance, almost half as many lakes within the city limits (some 180) as there are factory chimneys, not to mention generous amounts of greenery and open spaces.

In a class by itself is **Pyynikki,** a ridge that stretches from the centre of the city. At the foot of the ridge is an **open-air theatre** (*Pyynikin kesäteatteri*), famous for the revolving, bowl-like auditorium that seats 800. When a scene changes the backdrop stays put and the seating is rotated—from one beautiful view of lakes and forest to another.

Like Kuopio, Tampere boasts an observation tower, the **"Näsi Needle"** (*Näsinneulan Näkörtorni*), complete with observation deck, revolving restaurant and lovely views. It is situated on **Särkänniemi,** a peninsula jutting out into Lake Näsijärvi. From a spectacular vantage point over 550 feet high you can see how geography shaped Tampere. Most of the industry and much of the population is confined to the isthmus between the lakes, at one

point only about 1,500 feet wide. This is the place where the water from Lake Näsijärvi cascades into Lake Pyhäjärvi forming the **Tammerkoski Rapids,** the source of clean energy for the city's industry. Hämeenkatu, Tampere's main street, crosses the rapids by means of a bridge decorated with statues by Wäinö Aaltonen.

The Näsi Needle is only one feature of an extensive leisure complex at Särkänniemi. A **planetarium** presents special shows with a commentary in several languages, and an **aquarium** displays several hundred species of fish from around the world.

At the **Sara Hilden Art Museum** (*Sara Hildenin taidemuseo*), a handsome modern building complements a good collection of contemporary art. And in summer, a children's zoo and amusement park opens, just to be sure there's enough to see and do.

Authentic old steamers still dock across the little bay from Särkänniemi at Mustalahti harbour. They ply the romantic northern route across Lake Näsijärvi to VIRRAT, known as the **"Poet's Way"**, after the poet J.L. Runeberg, who did much of his work at RUOVESI, a town along the route. **81**

Lapland

Finland's frontier province stretches from just below the Arctic Circle almost to the Arctic Ocean. This enormous territory has only 200,000 inhabitants—and just as many reindeer. Most of Lapland's citizens are Finns who settled here in the last three decades, but there are some 4,000 residents of Lapp origin, about half of whom speak *saame*, the ancient Lappish language. They wear colourful costumes, which differ from region to region, and preserve the customs of their ancestors.

The reindeer provides the Lapps with their livelihood. A series of **reindeer roundups** are held in the autumn and winter, when herds are culled and the ears of reindeer calves are notched with the owner's special brand. The roundups are colourful sights, combining the more picturesque elements of a North American rodeo and a Finnish folk festival.

In summer reindeer generally migrate to the higher, cooler western region. But you can always be sure of seeing one,

Even if you don't run into a reindeer, you'll probably catch sight of a Lapp in folk dress.

along with a few Lapps in folk dress, at the Arctic Circle Cabin right by the airport that serves Rovaniemi, Lapland's capital, principal town and gateway city. Everywhere in Lapland there are lakes and rivers for fishing—or panning for gold. "Gold washing" makes a popular holiday pastime, especially at Tankavaara, far above the Arctic Circle. The town is the site of a Gold Washing Museum *(Kullanhuuhdontamuseo)*, which sponsors competitions in summer to see who can wash the most nuggets from the river.

While the vast outlying areas deserve to be explored in depth and at leisure, Rovaniemi (one hour and 40 minutes by air from Helsinki) makes a convenient starting place. Many tourists fly up for a day.

Rovaniemi

This neat community of about 30,000 was burned to the ground by retreating German forces in 1944 and had to be completely re-built. Alvar Aalto drew up the town plan, but unfortunately his attractive design doesn't adequately reflect the great wilderness region all around.

Aalto also designed **Lappia House** *(Lappia-talo)*, symbol of the city's phoenix-like post-war resurgence. Cultural events and congresses take place here. A section of the building is given over to the **Lapland Provincial Museum** *(Lapin maakuntamuseo)* and its prized possession—the crude carving of a moose, approximately 7,800 years old according to carbon dating. Fascinating displays of Lapp folk dress and crafts and a fine exhibition of the birds of Lapland round out the collection.

The **Lutheran Church** near by replaces a church that was erected on the site in 1632. By that date, Rovaniemi had become an important market town, due to its position at the

confluence of two rivers, Ounasjoki and Kemijoki (Finland's longest). Be sure to look at the notable murals inside the church, particularly the *Fountain of Life*, painted above the altar by Lennart Segerstråle. The Lapland landscape and peoples inspired this work, which replaces shepherds with reindeer herders.

The Kemijoki is still important to Rovaniemi. Great log booms are floated down it, and the electrical power the river generates is one of Lapland's exports. The region's rivers are a recreational asset, too, and there are a number of campgrounds and holiday cottage colonies along river banks in the Rovaniemi area.

The **Arctic Circle Cabin** (*Napapiirin Maja*), situated some 8 kilometres from town, stands right on the Arctic Circle. You can't possibly miss this geographical landmark: a sign in six languages indicates the precise spot. There is a restaurant, gift shop—even a resident reindeer herd. Have your picture taken cheek by jowl with a reindeer, or be photographed for posterity by the Arctic Circle sign. (Handsome certificates attesting to the circle crossing will be inscribed with your name.) There are always Lapp functionaries on hand to perform "baptismal" ceremonies: kneel on a reindeer skin, take a sip of reindeer milk—and you're officially a Lapp! The Rovaniemi tourist office will make all the necessary arrangements.

Arctic Nights, Northern Lights

The sun may shine on Nordic countries virtually round the clock in June, but an unrelenting winter darkness (*kaamos*) descends in December. At Ivalo in Lapland, for example, a month of perpetual night fades at last into twilight on January 9.

But in Helsinki winter isn't gloomy at all, even though daylight is in short supply, with no more than five hours on the shortest days. During the Christmas season, holiday lights transform the city into a fairyland. And the late-night sky can glow with the ghostly forms of the *aurora borealis* or Northern Lights.

A curtain of yellowish-green, violet or red undulates on the horizon, usually after 11 p.m. The play of light (at its most intense in March and April, September and October) is related to changes in the earth's magnetic field. Spots, patches and pulsating flames and rays are other manifestations of this unique natural phenomenon.

What to Do

Shopping

Finnish goods have been world famous for fine design since the 1950s, when talents like Tapio Wirkkala and Timo Sarpaneva reaped awards in international exhibitions. The hallmarks of the style they created are simplicity, utility and functional beauty. Finnish designers make good use of the country's

Modern glassware and textiles in colours inspired by nature help to make shopping in Finland a treat.

natural resources, working with wood, clay, textiles, and native semi-precious stones to produce objects of great beauty.

Where to Shop

Helsinki naturally offers the widest selection of merchandise, and every shopping expedition should begin in the capital. Head for the Finnish Design Centre at 19 Kasarmikatu, not far from Esplanadi.

You can see jewellery crafted from gold panned in Lapland, clean-lined furniture of native oak and birch and rugs in a rainbow of brilliant colours, often inspired by the traditional hand-knotted *ryijy* (rew-yew) of the countryside.

Many internationally known Finnish firms, such as Arabia (china), Marimekko (fabric and fashions) and Aarikka (wooden design items), have shops on one or both sides of the Esplanade. Finland's oldest and largest department store, Stockmann's, lures shoppers to Aleksanterinkatu, the parallel street. You'll find the other big stores—Alexei 13, Sokos, Elanto Centrum and Pukeva —in the same area. Look for all manner of craft and souvenir items among the stalls in Market Square.

Last, but not least, be sure to see the displays of *ryijy* rugs mounted by the Friends of Finnish Handicrafts *(Suomen käsityön ystävät),* a century-old organization. Both the little museum and a shop selling examples are housed in the Friends' Victorian headquarters, north of the central shopping area in the Meilahti district of town.

Shopping Hours

Hours vary slightly, but are mostly 9 a.m.–5 p.m., Monday to Friday, and 9 a.m.– 2 p.m. on Saturdays. Department stores open from 9 a.m. to 7 or 8 p.m., Monday–Friday, and till 3 or 4 p.m. on Saturdays. Shops in the Railway Station tunnel are generally open 10 a.m.–10 p.m., Monday to Saturday, and noon–10 p.m. on Sundays.

Tax Refunds for Visitors

The Finnish government levies a sales tax on most goods. Citizens of non-Scandinavian countries who make purchases at shops displaying the "Tax-free for Tourists" sticker will be refunded about 10% of the tax they pay. The purchases must not be used before leaving the country. The refund is made in cash at major points of departure (airports and seaports).

Best Buys

Boots are well-made, elegant (warm, too) and less expensive than in many other countries.

Candles in a wide range of colours and sizes light up every Finnish home.

Clothing, particularly sportswear and leisurewear designed by the internationally known Marimekko. Vuokko and others, is distinguished for bright colour, high quality and practically. Prices are generally competitive.

Fur coats and hats of native mink and blue fox can be purchased for prices that compare favourably with most countries.

Glassware and ceramics figure among Finland's most popular exports. Make your selection from the wide range of bowls, tumblers and tableware, all designed by distinguished craftsmen with international reputations.

Souvenirs include objects made of wood, *puukko* hunting **87**

knives and reindeer skins and antlers. Lapp crafts are popular too. Look for carvings made from reindeer bones, felt items and dolls.

Textiles for home decoration range from brightly patterned tablecloths and napkins to wall rugs, hangings, curtains, carpets and cushions. Cotton or linen fibres are favoured.

Wooden articles include all sorts of boxes, candle holders, jewellery and toys. Look for items made of juniper, a fragrant wood that doesn't lose its scent.

Sports

Finns enjoy sports and sporting events as much as any people in the world. Outdoor activities of all sorts are popular, particularly those that enable the sportsman to go back to nature.

First among winter sports is cross-country skiing, practised with equal enthusiasm in city parks and the winter wonderland of Lapland. When the snows melt and the midsummer sun shines bright and long, hikers take to the countryside and water-related activities come into their own, particularly sailing and swimming. For detailed information on sports in every season, contact the Finnish Tourist Board.

Skiing. Cross-country skiing is possible wherever there is snow, including frozen lakes and sea, even Helsinki parks— some of which have lighted tracks for night skiing. In Lapland, you can go ski touring from hut to hut during the long spring days, when snow is still plentiful. This is also the place to try ski-joring, a unique form of skiing in which you are towed along by a reindeer.

Downhill skiing has been growing in popularity. The top area is Lahti, site of many international events, but there are major centres at Kuopio, Jyväskylä, Tampere and Rovaniemi in Lapland. The runs at Hyvinkää (as well as the swimming pools, saunas and fitness centre) are popular with skiers from nearby Helsinki.

Swimming. Finns flock to beaches and lakes in summer, and swimming is one of the attractions. There is no better time for a refreshing dip than after a sauna (usually situated beside a lake). No visitor should avoid participating in

Competitors in cross-country ski race take a break, while daring sportsmen shoot the icy rapids.

In a land of flat, fertile fields, a bicycle's just the ticket for seeing the countryside up close; this birch-shaded path is in lively town of Kuopio.

this national rite if the opportunity presents itself (see p. 74).

Water-Skiing. This sport has grown in popularity in recent years, and there are many clubs all over Finland. Some offer weekly courses in season. For detailed information, contact the Finnish Water-Ski Association, Muurame kp 4.

Boats and Sailing. Finland's serrated coastline and thousands of offshore islands make for happy sailing. Yachts, motor boats and canoes can be hired in Helsinki and other major coastal towns. Hanko and Mariehamn in the Åland islands are particularly active yachting centres. A series of marked routes in Suur-Saimaa are ideal for small craft, and the Finnish Canoe Association organizes guided canoe tours in the area.

Tennis. The Finns have taken up tennis with a vengeance, and facilities for the booming sport have sprung up all over the country. Outdoor courts are in use from mid-May to September, and a

sizable number of indoor courts make year-round play possible. Tennis equipment can only rarely be hired, and players are advised to bring their own rackets.

Hiking. Finland's rolling terrain is well suited for hiking, and there are marked trails throughout the country. These vary in length and difficulty, allowing you to choose a route to match your endurance. It is unwise to strike out on your own, as there is always the risk of losing your way in the forests or on the fells.

Essential equipment includes durable boots, adequate maps (see p. 119) and a compass.

June through September is the best hiking time over most of the country.

Fishing. With thousands of large inland lakes and a long coastline, Finland is a fisherman's paradise. Finnish coastal waters have such a low salt content that it is quite common for saltwater fish to be found side by side with freshwater species. The most important salmon river, the Teno, forms the border with Norway. During spawning season, salmon swim up this river from the Arctic Ocean.

In winter many keen fishermen cut holes in the ice and keep on angling. A general **91** fishing permit, obtainable at any post office, is required, as well as a licence to fish the waters of a particular area (issued on the spot by hotels, campsites, etc.).

Riding. You can canter along country lanes or follow some of the bridle paths that have been laid out in rural areas. Riding clubs all over Finland hire out mounts, and many of them provide instruction in a variety of languages.

Cycling. One of the most pleasant ways to see Finland is from the seat of a bicycle. Several travel agents offer package tours which provide itineraries and include bicycle hire. Bicycle paths are to be found around Helsinki and Espoo, but the best cycling country is along the south coast and in the Åland islands and Saimaa region.

Nightlife

Helsinki provides its share of international entertainment, ranging from films shown in the original versions to excellent weekly concerts featuring the city's two orchestras and a prestigious array of guest artists. Works by Finland's greatest composer, Jean Sibelius, figure prominently in the repertoire. The biggest audiences gather in Finlandia Hall, and Temppeliaukio, the Rock Church, draws crowds as much for its innovative architecture as for the music.

The National Opera gives a staggering number of performances annually, many of them in the attractive little Helsinki opera house. A selection of plays staged in English and other foreign languages are avidly attended by multi-lingual Finns, so be sure to book seats in advance.

Finland's lively discotheques follow the usual international formula of music and dancing, with one exception, the *naisten-tanssit*. This is a dance organized especially for women on their way home from the office, usually from 4 p.m. Women, rather than men, take their pick of partners. Some discos also arrange evenings for women *(sekahaku)*. On these occasions men and women choose dancing partners freely. Note that Finnish establishments rarely charge admission, though you are expected to buy at least one drink.

Popular, too, are late-night restaurants with dancing. You'll see everything from the *polkka* to the *humppa*, a Finnish skipping step performed at a gallop.

Calendar of Events

Holiday celebrations enliven Finnish life all through the year. Festive occasions range from local folk gatherings to the joyous national revelry of Midsummer's Eve.

In addition, the Finnish government sponsors winter sports competitions and summer cultural festivals (Finland Festivals) country-wide. The series attracts participants from abroad, as well as the best of local talent. Festival events are deservedly popular with visitors and have an international reputation for excellence. Many programmes are free, and most include special activities for children.

January *January Market and Carnival,* Kuopio. A tradition since the 18th century. Held in Market Square.

February *Finlandia Ski Race.* This gruelling 47-mile race from Hämeenlinna to Lahti attracts several thousand skiers from nearly two dozen countries. Entry open to anyone on payment of a fee. Usually held towards the end of the month.

March	*Lady Day Church Festival,* Enontekiö. Lapps gather from far and wide to attend church services, followed by colourful reindeer events.
May 1	*Vappu* (May Day). This festival welcomes spring, beginning with all-night parties on April 30. Student celebrations are especially lively.
June	*Juhannus* (Midsummer Day). Finns make merry on the eve of the longest day of the year. Ceremonial bonfires are lit and people dance in the open air. The longest day reigns as a public holiday. Celebrated on the Saturday closest to June 24.
June/July	*Jyväskylä Arts Festival.* An important cultural event featuring exhibitions, concerts, theatrical and film presentations, seminars.
	Kuopio Dance and Music Festival. Everything from ballet to ballroom dancing. Some events are held out of doors in Market Square. The brass band competitions are a particular crowd-pleaser.
July	*Savonlinna Opera Festival.* One of the major Finnish cultural festivals. Performances are held throughout the month, with a cast of international stars.
July 27	*Sleepy-Heads Day,* Hanko/Hangö, Naantali. Someone with problems waking up in the morning is elected sleepy-head. Day-long celebrations follow (see p. 62).
August	*Turku Music Festival.* A classical music festival that includes some pop music concerts. In Finland's atmospheric oldest town.
	Tampere Theatre Festival. Indoor and outdoor performances—the latter in Tampere's famous revolving Pyynikin kesäteatteri.
August/September	*Helsinki Festival.* The premier national festival. Concerts, ballet, opera, theatre, art exhibits and literally hundreds of other events are staged in Finlandia Hall, the City Theatre and other auditoriums.
December 6	*Independence Day.* Windows all over Finland light up with candles in celebration of Finland's independence from Russia, declared December 6, 1917. Student processions also mark the occasion.

Dining and Drinks

Ferocious Vikings with appetites to match, hard-riding (and drinking) Cossacks, Lapp reindeer herders, French army officers and Russian and Swedish aristocrats have all added a pinch of pepper to Finland's culinary pot. As you might expect, the result is delicious*.

* For a comprehensive guide to dining in Finland, consult the Berlitz EUROPEAN MENU READER.

Where to Eat

Only at a *ravintola* (restaurant) can you sit down to a complete meal served by a waiter. Moreover, these are the only establishments permitted to offer strong beer and wine. A *baari* or *grilli* (snackbar) and *kahvila* (cafeteria) amount to more or less the same thing: coffee, softs drinks, weak beer, snacks and self-service. Incidentally, a cocktail bar in Finland is called an *American Bar* or *Pub*, never a *baari*.

During the summer (mid-May to end of August), many restaurants offer a special menu for tourists. Known as the *Finland Menu,* it features a selection of typical dishes. There are three price categories, which vary according to the establishment. Ask the tourist office for a list of restaurants participating in the scheme.

It is not customary to say "bon appétit"—or the Finnish equivalent—at the start of the meal, but it is usual to say thank you *(kiitos)* to your host at the end. And you will rarely go wrong in Finland by smiling, raising a glass and offering the local version of "Cheers": *Kippis!*

Meal Times

Lunch is served from 11 a.m. to 1 p.m., and Finns take their evening meal early, too—around 5 p.m. at home or from 7 p.m. in restaurants. As a rule, restaurants stay open at least until 11 p.m.; those with dancing, as late as 2 or 3 a.m. It's wise to book in advance.

Keep in mind that alcoholic drinks stronger than beer cannot be sold before noon. Finnish laws regarding drinking and driving are particularly strict and rigidly enforced (see **96** DRIVING p. 113).

Breakfast

A Finnish breakfast is a hearty meal. You'll generally be served fruit juice to start, then coffee or tea. Next come several varieties of bread and rolls with butter and jam, not to mention cheese, eggs and sausages.

Fish and Shellfish

Given the length of the seacoast and the numbers of offshore islands, it is not surprising that fish and seafood dominate the Finnish diet. And, of course, those 62,000 lakes yield a yearly harvest of trout, salmon, whitefish and other delicious freshwater varieties.

Like other Scandinavians, the Finns do wonderful things with Baltic herring *(silakka),* available all the year round. This small silvery fish can be fried, baked, charcoal-grilled or smoked—when it turns a golden colour. Salted or marinated, Baltic herring makes a popular first course, always accompanied by boiled potatoes and often by a schnapps. One hearty speciality, *silakkalaatikko,* combines Baltic herring and sliced potato in a casserole. A larger variety of herring *(silli)* is also widely served.

Muikku, a white freshwater fish found in certain Finnish lakes, is the main ingredient in *kalakukko* (see p. 76) and other special dishes from the province of Savo. But perhaps the best the *muikku* can provide is its roe *(muikunmäti)*. This is served Russian-style with chopped onions, pepper and fresh or sour cream. Toast or small pancakes called *blinit* (Russian *blinis*) and an ice-cold vodka schnapps are the inevitable accompaniments.

No foreigner should leave Finland without tasting salmon *(lohi)*. Enjoy it grilled, boiled, in soup or in pastry *(kulibjaka)*. Like many Finns, you may prefer salmon raw and very slightly salted *(graavilohi)*.

Finns regard the crayfish *(rapu*, plural *ravut)* as the supreme offering of rivers and lakes. This delicious crustacean is consumed with gusto and considerable ceremony from about the end of July to early September. Even the most dignified diners tuck bibs under their chins to tackle a plate of steaming crayfish.

Meat Dishes

For local flavour, try reindeer meat *(poro, poronliha)*. Lapps eat just about every part of the reindeer, except for the horns (which are used for other purposes). Most Finns are more selective, restricting themselves to such specialities as reindeer in cream sauce *(poronkäristys)* or cold smoked reindeer *(savustettua poronlihaa)* and reindeer tongue *(poronkieli)*, whether smoked *(savustettu)* or served with lemon sauce *(sitruunakastikkeen kera)*.

Game appears on menus in season: duck *(sorsa)*, pheasant *(fasaani)*, white ptarmigan *(riekko)*, hare *(jänis)*, bear *(karhu)* and elk *(hirvi, hirvipaisti)*. These dishes are enhanced by two products of the Finnish forests: a jam or jelly made from wild berries and one of 200 varieties of mushrooms *(sieniä, sienet)*.

Finnish Specialities

Many typical dishes are seldom served in restaurants, but you may come across *hernekeitto*, pea soup with pieces of pork, traditionally served on Shrove Tuesday. The soup, followed by a bun filled with almond paste and whipped cream, provides sustenance for weeks of Lenten fasting ahead.

Be sure to sample *kalakukko*, a regional speciality of Savo province. You'll see vendors at the Kuopio market selling this snack food—a thick loaf of rye bread baked with a filling of fish (usually *muikku* or perch) and pork, served sliced and spread with butter. From eastern Finland comes **97** another portable snack called *karjalanpiirakka*, a thin shell of rye dough stuffed with rice or potato. This Karelian speciality is eaten hot with a spread of chopped egg and butter.

Lakeside picnic takes shape as pancakes cook over an open fire.

Voileipäpöytä

Finland has its own version of that Scandinavian invention, the *smörgåsbord*. Here, as in other Nordic countries, you choose freely from a buffet table laden with dozens of dishes. Begin with some of the herring dishes, then return to the table for a sampling of fish

and seafood specialities, followed by reindeer and other cold meats, salads, mushrooms, etc. It is customary to make several trips to the buffet, eating a little at a time in the order suggested. You are invited to as many helpings as you can manage.

The *voileipäpöytä* also features a variety of warm dishes, but these are of secondary importance. There is usually cheese available, as well as some fruit.

Cheese

Finnish cheeses *(juusto)* compare favourably with the best of other countries. Emmental- and Edam-type cheeses rival their Swiss and Dutch counterparts, and Finnish Camembert is hardly distinguishable from the French. There is also a Finnish Cheddar *(juhla)*, as well as a blue-veined Roquefort-type *(aura)*.

The typically Finnish homemade cheeses are not readily available in restaurants. Ask at a cheese shop for *piimäjuusto* (buttermilk cheese) and *ilves* (a baked loaf-shaped cheese).

Sweets

Finns are fond of cakes and pastries, but these are mostly eaten as a snack with coffee, rather than after a meal. Blueberry pie *(mustikkapiirakka)* is one delicacy among dozens available in pastry shops (and less often in restaurants). The most popular desserts, available only during the summer months, are wild berries made sweet by the midnight sun: *lakka* (Arctic cloudberries—a sort of yellow raspberry with a delicate flavour), *karpalo* (cranberries) and *pihlajanmarja* (rowanberries).

Drinks

Coffee *(kahvi)* is so much in evidence in Finland that it must be considered the national drink. You will be offered countless cups—at breakfast, after lunch, in the afternoon, at dinner, even late at night, generally with pastries, cookies or cakes. However, tea *(tee)* is a very different matter, and few restaurants and cafés make it to English standards.

Finnish beer, a light lager served fairly cold, comes in three strengths: No. I *(ykkösolut)* is virtually a temperance drink, with only a trace of alcohol. No. III *(kolmosolut or keskiolut)*, a mild brew available in cafeterias, has a fairly low alcohol content. The relatively stronger No. IV *(nelosolut or A-olut*—with an "a" as in "father") is sold only in licenced restaurants. For rea- **99**

In the strawberry season, Finns find many uses for the fresh fruit.

sons best known to the government alcohol monopoly (Alko), there is no No. II *olut*.

Domestic wine made from berries and fruit is little more than a curiosity, but you may want to sample *Elysée*, a sparkling white wine made from currants. On the other hand, domestic liqueurs distilled from wild berries are widely appreciated. Ask for *Lakka* (yellow cloudberry liqueur), *Polar* (red cranberry), *Mesimarja* (red Arctic bramble) or *Vaapukka* (red raspberry).

Vodka, the most popular strong drink in Finland, is served either as a schnapps *(snapsi)* or mixed with juices, for instance lingonberry *(puolukkamehu)* or orange *(appelsiinimehu)*. An interesting aperitif, *Vodka Polar*, combines vodka with Polar liqueur. Finns do much of their toasting with the *Koskenkorva* brand, made smooth by the addition of a small amount of sugar. This vodka also has a slightly lower alcohol content than the rival *Dry Vodka*, exported under the *Finlandia* name. Remember that vodka should always be accompanied by some sort of food.

To Help You Order...

Could we have a table?	**Saisimmeko pöydän?**		
Do you have a set menu?	**Onko teillä päivän ateriaa?**		
I'd like...	**Haluaisin...**		

beer	**olutta**	mustard	**sinappia**
bread	**leipää**	pepper	**pippuria**
cheese	**juustotarjottimen**	potatoes	**perunoita**
coffee	**kahvia**	rice	**riisiä**
dessert	**jälkiruokaa**	salad	**salaattia**
fish	**kalaa**	salt	**suolaa**
fruit	**hedelmiä**	soup	**keittoa**
fruit juice	**hedelmämehua**	sugar	**sokeria**
ice-cream	**jäätelöä**	tea	**teetä**
meat	**liharuokia**	water	**vettä**
milk	**maidon**	wine	**viiniä**

...and Read the Menu

appelsiini	orange	**parsa**	asparagus
hauki	pike	**pekoni**	bacon
herneet	peas	**porkkanat**	carrots
hirvenliha	elk	**poronliha**	reindeer
kana	chicken	**porsas**	pork
kananmunat	eggs	**purjosipulit**	leeks
karhunliha	bear steak	**päärynä**	pear
karviaismarjat	gooseberries	**ravut**	crayfish
kolja	haddock	**retiisi**	radish
lammas	lamb	**riisipuuro**	rice pudding
lohi	salmon	**sampi**	sturgeon
luumut	plums	**siika**	whitebait
makkara	sausage	**silli**	herring
maksa	liver	**sipulit**	onions
mansikat	strawberries	**suolasilli**	pickled herring
naudanliha	beef	**tomaatit**	tomatoes
ohukkaat	pancakes	**vadelmat**	raspberries
oliivit	olives	**vasikka**	veal
omenat	apples	**vihreät pavut**	green beans

BLUEPRINT for a Perfect Trip

How to Get There

Although the fares and conditions described below have all been carefully checked, it is advisable to consult a travel agent for the latest information on fares and other arrangements.

From Great Britain

BY AIR: Non-stop flights leave daily from London (Heathrow) for Helsinki. Less frequent flights link Birmingham, Aberdeen, Glasgow and Manchester with Helsinki via Copenhagen. Other airports offer flights with a change at Heathrow, Amsterdam or Brussels. An excursion fare is available for a stay of six days to one month, as well as the APEX (Advance Purchase Excursion) fare, valid seven days to three months. The APEX fare must be booked one month before departure.

Charter Flights and Package Tours: At present, very few charter flights operate on this route. You could save money by choosing one of a wide range of full- or part-board packages. The Finnair Holiday Ticket, which you can purchase at home or in Finland, entitles you to one or two weeks' unlimited travel on the country's domestic air network.

BY SEA AND ROAD: Several combinations of land and sea travel will get you to Helsinki. If you want to come by ferry, you can travel from Felixstowe or Newcastle (summer only) to Gothenburg in Sweden. The journey takes about 24 hours. From Gothenburg the quickest route is via the E3 motorway to Stockholm, and from there by ferry to Helsinki (14 to 16 hours, year-round service). While both ferry and train services operate from Gothenburg to Stockholm, note that the trip by ferry takes a leisurely 57 hours, as opposed to 6 hours at most by train. Another possibility is to drive to Travemünde in northern Germany, and take the Finnjet high-speed car-and-passenger ferry to Helsinki, a journey of about 22 hours in the summer (26 hours in winter).

BY RAIL: You can travel from London to Helsinki by train via Ostend—Cologne—Hamburg—Stockholm or, alternatively, the Hook (Holland)—Bremen—Hamburg—Stockholm. Both trips total about 50 hours, including a 2-hour stopover in Stockholm. Sleepers and couchettes are available, but you must book well in advance. The Inter-Rail Card permits 30 days of unlimited rail travel in participating European countries to youths under 26 and women over 60 and men over 65. However, in the country of issue, 50% of the fare must be paid.

Within Finland, the Finnrail Pass gives unlimited travel for 8, 15, 22 days or one month; the Nordic Tourist Ticket allows unlimited travel in Finland, Denmark, Norway and Sweden.

From North America

There are direct flights to Helsinki from four cities in North America—Toronto (twice weekly), New York (daily except Tuesdays and Sundays), Los Angeles (twice weekly) and Seattle (once a week). Connecting flights are available daily from 30 major American cities, plus Montreal, Toronto, Vancouver and Winnipeg.

The major carriers offer several bargain fares. The APEX (Advance Purchase Excursion) fare must be booked and ticketed 21 days prior to departure (penalty for cancellation). The Excursion fare requires no advance booking or ticketing and carries no cancellation penalty.

Charter Flights and Package Tours: Finnair is currently featuring the Finnweekend—five days and four nights, including round-trip air transport from New York, hotel and breakfast. For those with more time, several GIT's (Group Inclusive Tours) may be combined with stays in Moscow and Leningrad, or the Scandinavian capitals. Travellers who prefer independent sightseeing may choose from an array of FIT's (Foreign Independent Tours) from two to nine days' duration.

When to Go

Summer days in Finland are long and sunny, but rarely uncomfortably warm. Best weather is usually in July, especially in Lapland, and during the midnight sun season (from June 6–July 5 in Rovaniemi). The Finnish winter is a time of great beauty, with snowy landscapes and spectacular northern lights displays, especially in the far north—but obviously, it's quite cold.

Average monthly temperatures in Helsinki:

	J	F	M	A	M	J	J	A	S	O	N	D
°F	21	21	25	37	48	57	63	61	52	41	34	27
°C	–6	–6	–4	3	9	14	17	16	11	5	1	–3

Planning Your Budget

To give you an idea of what to expect, here are some average prices in Finnish marks (mk). Naturally, these are approximate, as costs will always vary in different places and at different times. And inflation creeps relentlessly up.

Airport transfer. Bus from the airport to city air terminal 16 mk, taxi 90–100 mk.

Baby-sitters. 12 mk and up per hour (7.50 mk/hr extra per child).

Bicycle hire. 40 mk per hour.

Camping. * (modest) 23–35 mk for family with car and tent or caravan, ** 33–48 mk, *** 45–70 mk, 13–20 mk for electricity, all per day. Sauna (for family) 40–90 mk per hour (50 min.), public sauna 11–20 mk per person.

Car hire. *Ford Fiesta* 159 mk per day, 1.84 mk per km., 2,100 mk per week with unlimited mileage. *Volvo 340 1.7* 206 mk per day, 2.20 mk per km., 2,900 mk per week with unlimited mileage.

Cigarettes. 14 mk per packet of 20.

Entertainment. Cinema 30–35 mk, theatre 70–80 mk, opera 140 mk, nightclub 50 mk (35–50 mk at weekends).

Finn Cheques. 155 mk.

Helsinki Card. 1 day 65 mk, 2 days 90 mk, 3 days 110 mk. Children, 7–16 years, 35/45/55 mk.

Hotels (double room with bath per night). Luxury 820–1,080 mk, average 560–790 mk, moderate 420–630 mk (without bath 230–320 mk).

Restaurants. Lunch for 2, inexpensive 60–70 mk, moderate 80–100 mk, expensive 300 mk. Beer 18–23 mk, wine 13–15 mk per person.

Sauna. Hotel sauna 10 a.m.–2 p.m. 50 mk per person, from 2 p.m. 90 mk per person (before 10 a.m. the sauna is included in room price).

Shopping bag. Loaf of bread 6–8 mk, litre of milk 4.10 mk, kilo of cheese 40–50 mk, 10 eggs 10 mk, 250 grams of butter 10 mk, kilo of beefsteak 60–80 mk.

Taxi. Basic fare in Helsinki 11.50 mk (elsewhere 11 mk), 4.29 mk (1–2 persons), 5.15 mk (3–4 persons) per km., plus 6 mk from 6 p.m. till 6 a.m. and on Sundays. And from 10 p.m. to 6 a.m. an extra 12 mk must be paid.

Youth hostels. 28–90 mk per person (members) depending on category, sheets 20 mk, non-members additional payment 15 mk.

An A–Z Summary of Practical Information and Facts

> A star (*) following an entry indicates that relevant prices are to be found on page 105.
>
> Listed after some basic entries is the appropriate Finnish translation, usually in the singular, plus a number of phrases that should help you when seeking assistance.

A

ACCOMMODATION (see also CAMPING and YOUTH HOSTELS)

Hotels*. Most hotels and motels in Finland are comparatively new, so that standards tend to be high. Nearly one third of all hotel beds are in Helsinki, where the range of accommodation runs from a bunk in a youth hostel to a luxury room in an international-style hotel. Finnish Tourist Board offices in Finland and abroad supply the brochure *Hotels, Motels, Hostels,* which gives all the facilities provided.

To encourage visitors to come by car, the Government sponsors a special discount programme offering books of *Finn Cheques,* valid in more than 150 hotels throughout the country. These cheques can only be purchased outside Finland. They are good from June 1 to August 31. Further information is available from Finnish Tourist Board offices and travel agencies for Scandinavia abroad.

The Helsinki Hotel Booking Centre is at Asema-aukio 3, next to the Railway Station (tel. 0-171 133).

Summer hotels. These are usually student living quarters open only during June, July and August. Comfortable accommodation in modern buildings at attractive rates.

Farmhouses. A number of farmhouses take in guests, who have their meals with the family on a full-board basis and can participate in the work of the farm if they wish. Ask the Tourist Board for the brochure *Farm Holidays in Finland.*

Holiday cottages. Nearly 6,000 holiday cottages, ranging from humble huts to luxury villas, are available for rent nationwide. The brochure *Finn-vacations* covers all you need to know about this type of accommodation.

Information: Lomarengas (Holiday Chain). Museokatu 3, 00100 Helsinki 10; tel. (0) 441 346

Holiday villages. Finland has more than 200 holiday villages consisting of self-contained first-class bungalows in rustic settings. Some are open all year round and are excellent for winter-holiday stays. For further details, write to the Tourist Board for the brochure *Holiday Villages in Finland*.

Information can also be obtained from the tourist offices of towns in the area in which you wish to stay.

I'd like a single/double room.	**Haluaisin yhden hengen huoneen/kahden hengen huoneen.**
with bath/with shower	**jossa on kylpyhuone/jossa on suihku**
What's the rate per night?	**Paljonko se maksaa yöltä?**

AIRPORTS* *(lentokenttä).* Helsinki-Vantaa, Finland's main airport, is 20 kilometres north of the city centre. It's an attractive modern complex with restaurants, shops, car hire desks, a tourist information counter, bank (see under MONEY MATTERS) and other amenities, including a duty-free shop for departing passengers. Finnair buses leave the airport every 10–30 minutes (between midnight and 7 a.m. after every arrival only) for the 25-minute drive to the Helsinki air terminal in Töölönkatu, right by the Intercontinental and Hesperia hotels. For departing passengers, buses leave the city air terminal daily at about 10-minute intervals during rush hours (20–30 minutes at other times), between 5.50 a.m. and 10 p.m.

Domestic flights. The country has around 20 domestic airports, all served by Finnair. The *Finnair Holiday Ticket* entitles you to 15 days' unlimited air travel (for non-residents who produce a ticket to Finland by air, rail or sea). Special tourist tickets and weekend, family and group reductions are also available. "Midnight-sun flights" leave Helsinki for Lapland daily from mid-May to mid-July with a stop at Rovaniemi—an impressive night excursion with meals included. Air taxis can also be hired.

BABY-SITTERS* *(lastenkaitsija).* Many hotels and holiday centres will arrange baby-sitting for their guests. Local tourist offices can also furnish names of experienced sitters.

Can you get me/us a baby-sitter for tonight?	**Voitteko hankkia minulle/meille lastenkaitsijan täksi illaksi?**

B **BICYCLE HIRE***. Bikes can often be hired at youth hostels and tourist offices, hotels, campsites and resort villages, as well as from some shops selling sports equipment.

Cycling is a popular way of travelling in Finland. There are several planned bicycle tours to choose from, covering for instance east and west Uusimaa (south, around Helsinki), Great Saimaa, the central lakes and the Åland islands.

If you would like to take an organized tour, ask for further details at the local tourist office.

C **CAMPING*** *(leirintä)*. There are some 350 campsites, 200 of which belong to the Finnish Travel Association *(Suomen Matkailuliitto)*. Sites are indicated by the international blue-and-white sign with a pictograph of a tent inside the letter "C", and graded by stars from one to three, the best offering riding, water-skiing, rowing and fishing. The Finnish camping season starts around the end of May in the south and lasts into September. In northern Lapland, the season is only about two months long. An international or Finnish camping card is required—obtainable at the sites. The Tourist Board's brochure *Camping sites and youth hostels* gives details on sites and camping in Finland. You can also contact the Finnish Travel Association, Camping Department, at Mikonkatu 25, SF-00100 Helsinki 10.

In Helsinki, a large camping ground at Rastila, 13 kilometres east of the city centre, is open from mid-May to mid-September.

Ask permission to camp on private property or outside recognized campsites. It is forbidden to light fires in the countryside; bring a camping stove if you intend to cook. Signs reading *kulovaroitus* (forest fire warning) and *kulohälytys* (forest fire alarm) are posted in areas where there may be danger.

May we camp here? **Voimmeko leiriytyä tänne?**

CAR HIRE*. See also DRIVING. The major international agencies are represented in Finland. Tourist information offices have lists of local firms. Otherwise, look under "Autovuokraamoja" or "Biluthyrning" in the yellow pages of the telephone directory.

To hire a car, you must show a valid driving licence from your country of residence. You should be at least 21 years old (25 for some firms). Most agencies require a cash deposit based on the estimated rental charge, but this condition is often waived for holders of major credit cards. The rates on page 105 include third-party insurance. Cars hired in Finland can generally be taken into the U.S.S.R., but additional Soviet insurance must be purchased beforehand.

CIGARETTES, CIGARS, TOBACCO* *(savukkeet, sikarit, tupakka).* **C**
A wide variety of brands, mostly British and American makes manu-
factured under licence, are sold at tobacconists, in kiosks, supermar-
kets and grocery stores.

I'd like a packet of...	**Haluaisin rasian...**
filter-tipped	**suodatinsavukkeita**
without filter	**ilman suodatinta**
I'd like some matches.	**Haluaisin tulitikkuja.**

CLOTHING. Light clothing can be worn in summer, though sweaters
and pullovers prove useful for chilly evenings—particularly on the
islands and in Lapland. Warm woollen clothing is recommended in
winter, with a wind-proof outer layer for skiing, skating and other outdoor sports; adequate hats, gloves and boots are essential.

In Helsinki and other large towns, better hotels and restaurants
insist on jacket and tie for men. Resort areas, however, are quite infor-
mal, and in summer shorts and bathing suits are commonly seen in
restaurants and cafés during daytime.

COMMUNICATIONS

Post offices can be identified by the words *Posti—Post.* Mailboxes are
painted yellow with the traditional post-horn in black. You also buy
stamps at stationery shops, hotels (a small extra charge is sometimes
made), railway stations and from yellow stamp machines.

Post office **hours** are generally from 9 a.m. to 5 p.m., Monday to Friday. Helsinki's main post office (see below) also keeps those hours for
ordinary postal services, but is open till 6 p.m. on Mondays in winter.

Poste restante (general delivery). In Helsinki, this is taken care of by
the main post office at:

Mannerheimintie 11, SF-00100 Helsinki 10

from 8 a.m. to 10 p.m. on weekdays, 11 a.m. to 10 p.m. on Sundays.

In other towns, specify the main post office: *Pääpostitoimisto.*

Telegrams *(sähke)* are handled by the Post Office, but hotel reception-
ists will also help in sending cables.

Telephone *(puhelin).* Most countries can be dialled direct. See the
white pages of the Helsinki telephone directory for instructions. **109**

C (Long-distance calls are cheaper between 5 p.m. and 7 a.m. and on weekends.)

Some area codes: Helsinki 90, Oulu 981, Tampere 931, Turku 921.

Some useful numbers (Helsinki):

Inquiries: Helsinki 012, national 020, international 92 020
Telephone rates for calls abroad: 92 023
Telegrams: 021
News in English: 040
"Helsinki Today" (programme of events): 058

Where's the (nearest) post office?	**Missä on (lähin) postitoimisto?**
A stamp for this letter/this postcard, please.	**Saisinko postimerkin tähän kirjeeseen/tähän postikorttiin?**
express (special delivery)	**pikalähetyksenä**
airmail	**lentopostissa**
registered	**kirjattuna**
poste restante (general delivery)	**poste restante**
Have you received any mail for…?	**Onko tullut mitään postia nimellä …?**
I want to send a telegram to…	**Haluan lähettää sähkeen…**
Can I use your telephone?	**Saanko käyttää puhelinta?**
Can you get me this number?	**Saisinko puhelun tähän numeroon?**
reverse-charge (collect) call	**vastapuhelu**
personal (person-to-person) call	**henkilöpuhelu**

COMPLAINTS. Since tourist services are of a high order and the average Finn is both friendly and courteous, few visitors have cause to complain. If you feel you have been overcharged in a shop or restaurant, ask to see the manager, who will probably settle the matter. If you fail to get satisfaction, contact the local tourist office. Criminal complaints should, of course, be referred to the police.

CONSULATES, EMBASSIES, LEGATIONS (*konsulaatti, suurlähetystö, lähetystö*)

Australia and New Zealand	Embassy Sergels Torg 12, 10342 Stockholm; tel. (990-46-8) 24 46 60
Canada	Embassy, Pohjoisesplanadi 25 B, 00100 Helsinki 10; tel. (90) 171 141

Eire	Legation, Linnég. 76, Stockholm; tel.: (990-46-8) 24 39 50
Great Britain	Consulate and embassy, Uudenmaankatu 16–20, 00120 Helsinki 12; tel. (90) 647 922
South Africa	Legation, Rahapajankatu 1A 5, 00160 Helsinki 16; tel. (0) 658 288
U.S.A.	Consulate and embassy, Itäinen Puistotie 14, 00140 Helsinki 14; tel (90) 171 931

CONVERTER CHARTS. For fluid and distance measures, see page 114. Finland uses the metric system.

Temperature

Length

Weight

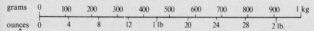

CUSTOMS *(tulli)* **and ENTRY REGULATIONS.** See also under DRIVING. Most visitors—including citizens of Great Britain, the U.S.A., Canada, Eire, Australia and New Zealand—need only a valid passport to enter Finland. British subjects can enter on the simplified Visitor's Passport. You are generally entitled to stay in Finland for up to three months without a visa. (This period includes the total time spent in Finland, Denmark, Iceland, Norway and Sweden in any six-month period.)

Entry formalities are minimal, consisting of a routine document check. Customs operates on the honour system, with occasional spot

C inspections. Here's what you can take into Finland duty free and, when returning home, into your own country:

Into:	Cigarettes	Cigars	Tobacco	Spirits	Wine
Finland*	200 or (400) or	250 g. or (500 g.) or	250 g. (500 g.)	1 l.	and 1 l.
Australia	250 or	250 g. or	250 g.	1 l.	or 1 l.
Canada	200 and	50 and	900 g.	1.1 l.	or 1.1 l.
Eire	200 or	50 or	250 g.	1 l.	and 2 l.
N. Zealand	200 or	50 or	250 g.	1.1 l.	and 4.5 l.
S. Africa	400 and	50 and	250 g.	1 l.	and 2 l.
U.K.	200 or	50 or	250 g.	1 l.	and 2 l.
U.S.A.	200 and	100 and	**	1 l.	or 1 l.

* The figures in parentheses are for non-European residents.
** a reasonable quantity

Travellers can bring in goods for a value of up to 1,500 mk duty free, exclusive of personal possessions.

Currency restrictions. There are no restrictions for tourists on the import of currency to Finland. You can export Finnish marks and foreign currencies up to the equivalent of what you brought in.

I've nothing to declare.   **Minulla ei ole mitään tullattavaa.**
It's for my personal use.   **Se on henkilökohtaiseen**
                             käyttööni.

D **DRIVING IN FINLAND.** You can bring your car into Finland if you have a valid driving licence and a national identity sticker displayed on the back of the car. A temporary import permit good for up to one year will be issued at the border. It is not allowed to lend a foreign-registered car to a person resident in Finland. Selling or transferring the vehicle without paying duty is illegal, and anyone doing so risks having it confiscated. The green insurance card is not obligatory for **112** motorists from countries belonging to the green-card system, but recommended in case of traffic accidents. Use of seat belts is compulsory. Motorcycle drivers and their passengers must wear crash helmets. All vehicles must have dipped headlights switched on at all times, even in broad daylight.

Driving conditions. Drive on the right, pass on the left, and use the horn only in emergencies. Traffic is generally light on Finnish roads, and even in and around Helsinki driving is difficult only in the morning and evening rush hours. Main roads are good throughout the country, but many secondary roads are unsurfaced. Winter tires are obligatory from December 1 to the end of February. Spikes are forbidden from April 1 to October 15 in southern Finland, from May 1 to September 30 in the north. In winter (September 1 to April 30), headlights must be used at all times. In many parts of southern Finland, elk wander out onto roads at dusk and cause accidents—use caution when driving through areas posted with elk pictographs.

Speed limits (mostly indicated by signs) vary, ranging from 60 to 80, 100 and 120 kilometres per hour, depending on the category of road and the density of traffic. Where speed limits are not posted, the basic limit is 80 kph (50 mph). The limit in urban areas is usually 50 kph (31 mph). Cars towing caravans (trailers) must not exceed 80 kph.

Drinking and driving. Perhaps the most important rule to remember while driving in Finland is to abstain from drinking any alcohol whatsoever. Finnish laws for drinking and driving are among the strictest in the world: 0.5⁰/₀₀ (per thousand) alcohol in the blood (one glass of beer or wine) is considered driving under the influence. Conviction always results in heavy fines and/or jail sentences.

Traffic police. Finnish roads are patrolled by the national mobile police *(liikkuva poliisi)*, which use marked and unmarked cars, as well as a number of helicopters. They patrol main roads vigilantly and are invariably courteous and helpful to drivers in difficulty—as long as the trouble isn't alcohol-related.

Breakdowns. The Automobile and Touring Club of Finland *(Autoliitto)* operates a 24-hour service telephone number in Helsinki that will give you the necessary information on garages of duty to come to your rescue in case of breakdown (see below). Elsewhere in the country, the Helsinki number can be contacted, and they'll give information on local garages, etc. If you are involved in an accident, report to the Finnish Motor Insurance Bureau *(Liikennevakuutusyhdistys)* before having major repairs done. If you injure or run over a reindeer or an elk, it must be reported to the nearest police station.

D Automobile and Touring Club service telephone number: (0) 694 0496

Finnish Motor Insurance Bureau: Bulevardi 28, 00120 Helsinki 12; tel. (0) 19 251

Fuel and oil *(polttoaine; öljy)*. Normal, super and diesel fuel are sold by the litre at service stations and garages. Service stations are numerous, but, in Finland as in most countries, more likely to be found on main roads and in towns than deep in the countryside. Service stations usually open from 7 a.m. to 9 p.m. (some close earlier on Sundays), garages from 7 a.m. to 4 p.m. on weekdays.

Fluid measures

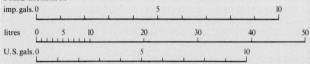

Distances. Here are some approximate road distances in kilometres between Helsinki and several major centres and border points:

Jyväskylä	275	Rovaniemi	835
Karigasniemi	1,265	Savonlinna	336
Kilpisjärvi	1,205	Tampere	175
Kuopio	394	Tornio	745
Kuusamo	810	Turku (Åbo)	165
Nuorgam	1,340	Vaalimaa	185
Oulu	615	Vaasa (Vasa)	415

To convert kilometres to miles:

Road signs. Most road signs are the standard pictographs used throughout Europe. However, you may encounter these written signs:

Aja hitaasti	Drive slowly
Ajo sallittu omalla vastuulla	Drive at own risk
Aluerajoitus	Local speed limit
Heikko tienreuna	Soft shoulders
Irtokiviä	Loose gravel
Kapea silta	Narrow bridge
Kelirikko	Frost damage
Kokeile jarruja	Test your brakes

Koulu	School
Liukas tie	Slippery road
Lossi	Ferry
Porovaara	Beware of reindeer
Perusnopeus	Basic speed limit
Uusi päällyste	Newly surfaced road
Tietyö	Road works

(international) driving licence	**(kansainvälinen) ajokortti**
car registration papers	**rekisterikirja**
green card	**vihreä kortti**
Are we on the right road for…?	**Viekö tämä tie …?**
Can I park here?	**Voiko tähän pysäköidä?**
Fill the tank please.	**Tankki täyteen, olkaa hyvä.**
super/normal	**korkeaoktaanista/tavallista**
Check the oil/tires/battery, please.	**Tarkistakaa öljy/renkaat/akku, olkaa hyvä.**
I've had a breakdown.	**Autooni on tullut vika.**
There's been an accident.	**On sattunut onnettomuus.**

For further information on motoring in Finland, contact the Automobile and Touring Club at:

Kansakoulukatu 10, 00100 Helsinki 10; tel. (0) 694 0022, telex 124839 autoclub sf

ELECTRIC CURRENT. The electric current throughout Finland is **E** 220-volt, 50-cycle A.C. Plugs are the round-pronged European type, and travellers with electric razors, irons, hair dryers and similar devices equipped with flat-pronged British or North American style plugs will need an adaptor.

I'd like an adaptor.	**Haluaisin välikappaleen pistorasiaan.**

EMERGENCIES. Depending on the nature of the emergency, refer to separate entries in this section of the book, such as CONSULATES, EMBASSIES AND LEGATIONS, HEALTH AND MEDICAL CARE, POLICE, etc. Hotel staff are prepared to assist in emergencies, as are local tourist offices and police. In Helsinki, you can call 000 free from any telephone to report police, fire and medical emergencies. In other towns, hotels and tourist offices keep lists of local emergency numbers (which are also listed in the first pages of telephone directories).

G **GUIDES and INTERPRETERS** *(opas; tulkki).* You can hire qualified guides through local tourist offices and travel agencies, or, in Helsinki, from the Guide Booking Centre (trained guides in some 15 languages; congress assistance):

Lönnrotinkatu 7, 00120 Helsinki; tel. (0) 601966, telex 125413 hotke sf

For interpreters, look in the yellow pages of the telephone directory under "Tulkkeja".

H **HEALTH and MEDICAL CARE.** To be at ease, make sure your health insurance policy covers any illness or accident while on holiday. Your travel agent or insurance company at home will be able to advise you. Finland has reciprocal health agreements with the Nordic countries, covering medical care and doctors' fees. There are also similar agreements with Britain.

The quality of medical service in Finland is very high. All hospitals have doctors—many speak English—on duty 24 hours a day. In Helsinki, you can call 000 or 181000 around the clock for a doctor, or go directly to the emergency ward at Meilahti Hospital *(Meilahden sairaala),* affiliated with the Helsinki University Central Hospital, Haartmaninkatu 4; tel. (0) 4711.

Tap water *(vesi)* is perfectly safe to drink everywhere in the country. All restaurants serve inexpensive mineral water *(kivennäisvesi).*

Pharmacies. A pharmacy *(apteekki)* in Finland is strictly a dispensary (for cosmetics, etc., you must go to a *kemikaalikauppa).* Many medicines which can be bought over the counter in other countries are available only on prescription in Finland. Chemists are open during normal shopping hours. After hours, a notice indicating the addresses of emergency pharmacies is posted in the window.

Where's the nearest (all-night) pharmacy?	**Missä on lähin (päivystävä) apteekki?**
I need a doctor/dentist.	**Tarvitsen lääkäriä/hammaslääkäriä.**
I have a pain here.	**Minulla on kipuja tässä.**

HEALTH FARMS and SPAS. Finland has an exceptional number of specialized establishments offering rest cures, fitness programmes and physical therapy tailored to individual needs. The farms and spas are situated in areas of great natural beauty, whether beside the sea or inland in a forest setting. There are several possibilities within a 30-mile (50-km.) radius of Helsinki, as well as others in the vicinity of Turku, Naantali, Savonlinna and so forth. Facilities range from saunas, hair-dressers and beauticians to tennis courts, golf course, jogging tracks, private beach or swimming pool and crosscountry skiing trails in the winter season.

Rates are normally quoted per night, with discount of up to 50% for children under the age of 11 or 12. Generally, full board terms are optional and include, on request, meal plans for dieters and vege-tarians.

General fitness programmes feature a host of activities to get you in shape, from gymnastics and water-exercises to hikes through the countryside. Guest may also follow a course of treatment under medical supervision. All the spas have qualified doctors and nurses on their staff. Balneotherapy is recommended for insomnia, rheumatic pain and skin problems, among other complaints. Massage promotes general relaxation, increased mobility and better fluid circulation. Heat treatments and mud packs improve blood circulation, relieve pain and aid in relaxation, while traction, light and electric stimulation treatments may also be prescribed, according to the individual case.

For further details, together with an up-to-date list of health farms and spas including prices and booking information, consult the near-est office of the Finnish Tourist Board or a travel agent specialized in Scandinavian holidays.

HELSINKI CARD *(Helsinki-kortti)*. The Helsinki Tourist Associa-tion offers *Helsinki Cards* that grant free entrance to museums, free travel on the blue city buses, on trams, underground (subway) and boats, tour reductions, hotel-rate discounts, etc. The card is valid for periods of one, two or three days, and can be purchased in the Hotel Booking Center next to the Railway Station, at certain hotels, some travel agencies and the Helsinki City Tourist Office.

HITCH-HIKING *(liftaaminen)*. Not as common as in some coun-tries, thanks to a good public-transport system.

LANGUAGE. Finland has two official languages, Finnish *(suomi—* which forms part of the Finno-Ugric family), spoken by around 93% of the population, and Swedish *(svenska* or, in Finnish, *ruotsi)*, used by around 6%. Many Finns are bilingual, especially in Helsinki. English is the foreign language most studied by Finns; German is also widely spoken.

L   Courses in Finnish for foreigners are arranged by the Ministry of Education *(Opetusministeriö)* at:

Pohjoisranta 4A, SF-00170 Helsinki

or write to the Council for Instruction of Finnish for Foreigners *(Suomen kielen ulkomaalaisopetus)* at:

Fabianinkatu 33, SF-00170 Helsinki

The Berlitz phrase book FINNISH FOR TRAVELLERS covers most situations you are likely to encounter in Finland; also useful is the Finnish-English/English-Finnish pocket dictionary, containing a special menu-reader supplement.

Here are a few words to get you going (see also p. 126):

Do you speak English?	**Puhutteko englantia?**
good morning	**hyvää huomenta**
good afternoon	**hyvää päivää**
good evening	**hyvää iltaa**
good night	**hyvää yötä**
hello	**hei**
good-bye	**näkemiin**

LAUNDRY and DRY-CLEANING *(pesula; kuivapesula)*. All hotels can arrange for laundry and dry-cleaning to be done. Larger hotels often return both on the same day if the garments are handed in early enough. There's usually an additional charge—up to 50%—for fast service. Laundry and dry-cleaning establishments are found in all major Finnish towns, and are listed in the yellow pages of the telephone directory under "Pesulaitoksia" and "Tvätt- och Strykinrättningar".

When will it be ready?	**Milloin se on valmis?**
I must have this for tomorrow morning.	**Minun täytyy saada tämä huomisaamuksi.**

LOST PROPERTY *(löytötavaratoimisto)*. Honesty is taken for granted in Finland, and in hotels, restaurants, cafés, etc., your coat, camera or wallet will be kept and put aside if you leave it behind. The first thing to do when you discover you have lost something is to **118** retrace your steps. In Helsinki, the police lost property office is located at Päijänteenkatu 12A. There are left luggage offices at the Railway Station and at the bus terminal off Simonkatu.

I've lost my wallet/handbag/ passport.

Olen kadottanut lompakkoni/ käsilaukkuni/passini.

MAPS. Street plans and small-scale maps of Finland can be obtained free at local tourist offices. When hiking or walking in the vast uninhabited areas, don't forget to bring a detailed map, as well as a compass—you can go literally hundreds of miles without meeting a soul.

The maps in this guide were prepared by Falk-Verlag, Hamburg, who also publish a city map of Helsinki.

I'd like a road map of this region.

Haluaisin tämän seudun tiekartan.

a street plan of...

...n kaupungin kartta

MEETING PEOPLE. Finns sometimes seem reserved, but there isn't a more hospitable people. They like to be on a first-name basis with acquaintances and are quick to invite visiting business associates and other foreigners to share in the sauna ritual.

Farmhouse holidays (see ACCOMMODATION) provide tourists with an opportunity to see how families live in Finland. Travel agencies can organize professional study tours, usually on a group basis, in which contacts are arranged with specialists in different fields and professions.

MONEY MATTERS

Currency. The Finnish mark—*markka* (but 2 *markkaa,* abbr. *mk*)—is divided into 100 *penniä* (but 1 *penni,* abbr. *p*). Although 1, 2, 3 and 4 p are quoted in prices, all sums are rounded off to the nearest 5 or 10 p at cash counters.

Coins: 5, 10, 20 and 50 p, 1, 5 and 10 mk.

Banknotes: 10, 50, 100, 500 and 1,000 mk.

For currency restrictions, see CUSTOMS AND ENTRY REGULATIONS.

Banking hours are normally from 9.15 a.m. to 4.15 p.m., Monday to Friday.

The currency-exchange office at Helsinki Railway Station is open from 11 or 11.30 a.m. to 6 p.m. daily.

M   The Helsinki Airport bank: 7 a.m. to 11 p.m. daily.

A bank at South Harbour, the Olympia boat terminal *(Olympiaterminaali)* is open from 9 to noon and 3 to 6 p.m. daily.

Credit cards and traveller's cheques. Major credit cards are accepted in most hotels and restaurants, service stations, department stores and shops. Internationally recognized traveller's cheques are easily cashed, although you may need your passport for identification. Other traveller's cheques can only be cashed in banks or currency-exchange offices. Eurocheques are widely accepted in Finland.

I want to change some pounds/dollars.	**Haluaisin vaihtaa puntia/dollareita.**
Do you accept traveller's cheques?	**Otatteko vastaan matkasekkejä?**
Can I pay with this credit card?	**Voinko maksaa tällä luottokortilla?**

N   **NEWSPAPERS and MAGAZINES** *(sanomalehdet; aikakauslehdet).* The principal daily newspapers are *Helsingin Sanomat* and *Uusi Suomi* in Finnish and *Hufvudstadsbladet* in Swedish. Hotel news-stands and railway station kiosks carry the most widely read British and continental papers, including the *International Herald Tribune,* usually on the day after publication. *Time* and *Newsweek* are also readily available, along with other foreign publications, at the Academic Bookstore *(Akateeminen kirjakauppa)* on the North Esplanade in Helsinki and at some kiosks. *Helsinki this week,* published by Helsinki Tourist Association, gives information in English, Swedish and German, and is distributed free in hotels. An attractive Government-sponsored magazine, *Look at Finland,* which carries many articles about cultural and tourist attractions, is sold at Suomalainen Kirjakauppa (Aleksanterinkatu 23) and at the Finnish Tourist Board office in Helsinki. In Helsinki, dial 040 for a news summary in English.

Have you any English-language newspapers?	**Onko teillä englanninkielisiä sanomalehtiä?**

P   **PHOTOGRAPHY.** Most of the international brands of film are available in camera shops in Finland. Visitors are allowed to bring in a reasonable amount of film duty free for personal use.

I'd like some film for this camera.	**Haluaisin filmin tähän kameraan.**	**P**
black-and-white film	**mustavalkoisen filmin**	
colour prints	**värifilmin**	
colour slides	**diafilmin**	

POLICE. See also EMERGENCIES. Finnish police wear dark-blue uniforms. In summer, grey shirts with blue shoulder straps replace jackets. Police cars are also dark blue, with POLIISI written on the side in large white letters. Highways are patrolled by the mobile police (*liikkuva poliisi*), a first-rate para-military national force. Many Finnish policemen speak English or other non-Scandinavian languages, particularly those on duty in resort and tourist areas.

Where is the nearest police station?	**Missä on lähin poliisiasema?**

PUBLIC HOLIDAYS (*pyhäpäivä*). Both Christian and secular holidays are scrupulously observed, with shops, banks and businesses closing all day.

Jan. 1	*uudenvuodenpäivä*	New Year's Day
May 1	*vappu*	May Day
Dec. 6	*itsenäisyyspäivä*	Independence Day
Dec. 24	*jouluaatto*	
Dec. 25	*joulupäivä*	Christmas
Dec. 26	*tapaninpäivä*	
Movable Dates:	*loppiainen*	Epiphany (always a Saturday)
	pitkäperjantai	Good Friday
	toinen pääsiäispäivä	Easter Monday
	Kristuksen taivaaseen-astumisen päivä	Ascension (always a Saturday)
	helluntain valmistuspäivä	Whit Saturday
	juhannuspäivä	Midsummer Day (the Saturday nearest to June 24)
	pyhäinpäivä	All Saints' Day (the Saturday nearest to Nov. 1)

R **RADIO and TV.** The Finnish Broadcasting Company operates the national radio and television service. BBC World Service and Voice of America can also be picked up.

The country has three TV channels. Imported programmes are broadcast in the original language with subtitles in Finnish.

S **SAUNAS*.** See also page 74. Because virtually every Finnish family has access to a private sauna—there are around one million in the country—commercial saunas are not common. However, you can enjoy a sauna at most hotels, motels and holiday villages and at many campsites. A sauna may be hired for parties, complete with fireplace, grilled sausages and drinks.

T **TIME DIFFERENCES.** Local time is East-European Time, two hours ahead of Greenwich Mean Time. In summer, clocks are set one hour ahead (GMT+3).

	New York	London	**Helsinki**	Jo'burg	Sydney	Auckland
winter:	5 a.m.	10 a.m.	**noon**	noon	9 p.m.	11 p.m.
summer:	5 a.m.	10 a.m.	**noon**	11 a.m.	7 p.m.	9 p.m.

What time is it, please?　　　　　**Paljonko kello on?**

TIPPING. Tipping is not a widespread habit in Finland. A service charge of 14% (15% on weekends and public holidays) is automatically added to restaurant and bar bills. Waiters and taxi drivers don't expect tips, but a few extra coins for good service is customary. Barbers and hairdressers are not tipped. Some further suggestions:

Porter, per bag	5 mk (optional)
Doorman, hails cab	5 mk
Lavatory attendant	2 mk
Hat check	3–5 mk

TOURIST INFORMATION OFFICES. The Finnish Tourist Board distributes useful maps and brochures free, and provides suggestions for all sorts of unusual holidays. It maintains offices in some major cities abroad:

Great Britain   Finnish Tourist Board UK Office, 66/68 Haymarket, London SW1Y 4RF; tel. (071) 839-4048

U.S.A.   Finnish Tourist Board NA Office, 655 Third Avenue, New York, NY 10017; tel. (212) 370-5540

The Finnish Tourist Board's information office in Helsinki is at Unioninkatu 26, 00130 Helsinki; tel. 174 631.

   Finnish cities and most small towns have their own tourist information office, almost always centrally located on the main street or market square and marked by a large letter **i** on a green background. The main information office in Helsinki is the City Tourist Office at Pohjoisesplanadi 19; tel. 169 3757.

Where is the tourist office?   **Missä on matkailutoimisto?**

TRANSPORT (see also CAR HIRE)

City transport. Buses *(bussi)* and trams *(raitiovaunu)* operate throughout Helsinki and suburbs. Service is frequent and vehicles are modern. On buses and trams marked with a black "E" on a yellow background, the fare is paid to the driver. Books of multi-trip tickets good for unlimited travel on buses and trams are available. A *tourist ticket* valid for 24 hours can be purchased for use on all public transport, including a round trip on tram 3 T, with loudspeakers commenting on the sights (in English, German and Swedish) during summer (excluding rush hours).

   A metro (underground/subway) line operates from Kamppi via Rautatientori (Railway Square) to Itäkeskus in the eastern suburbs. Bus and tram tickets are valid also for the metro.

   With the Helsinki Card, travel is free on city buses, on trains and on the metro.

Taxis. Finnish taxis are usually diesel sedans marked unmistakably with the word "Taksi". A yellow roof light is turned on when the car is free. Vehicles are metered and have radios. There's a surcharge at weekends and at night. Taxis can be hailed in the street or from a **123**

T rank. If you call for one by phone (see telephone directories under "Taksiasemat"/"Taxistationer"), drivers are allowed to flip on the meter at the point they get the call (companies dispatch the nearest driver), so a considerable sum can mount up before you've even started. A service charge is included in the fare, and drivers don't expect a tip (but a few extra coins for good service is customary).

Coaches. Both regular and express services are convenient and an inexpensive means of transport all over the country. In Helsinki, coaches leave from the central bus station off Simonkatu behind the *Lasipalatsi* (Glass Palace). There are reductions for families and groups. Children under four travel free, from four through 11 for half fare. Information on timetables, tickets, etc., is available at any coach station. A *Lapland tourist ticket*, valid in both Finnish and Norwegian Lapland, may be purchased.

Trains (*juna*). The Finnish State Railways operate between major cities and towns as far north as Kemijärvi in Lapland. Service is good, and trains are clean and comfortable. First-class express trains run between major cities such as Helsinki and Tampere. First- and second-class seats may be reserved for a small extra charge; express-train seats must be booked in advance. Age limits for children are the same as on coaches. There are special group, family and *tourist tickets* (which can be combined with travel by coach, plane and boat) available. *Eurail-passes* and *Inter-Rail tickets* (see HOW TO GET THERE, p. 102) are valid in Finland. The *Finnrail Pass* entitles you to unlimited travel for periods of 8, 15 or 22 days or one month in first or second class (for foreign visitors only; bring your passport when purchasing the ticket). The *Nordic Tourist Ticket* permits 21 days of unlimited rail travel in Denmark, Finland, Iceland, Norway and Sweden.

Boat services. For Korkeasaari, boats leave from Kauppatori, Pohjoisranta and Hakaniemenranta (east Helsinki); alternatively, there's a toll bridge via Mustikkamaa island. Suomenlinna is reached by boat from Kauppatori; Pihlajasaari by motorboat from Merisatamanranta; Seurassaari by motorboat from Kauppatori. Åland ferries leave from Turku and Naantali. Trips to Leningrad must be booked at least two weeks in advance; there are day trips from Lappeenranta to Vyborg with connections to Leningrad.

I want a ticket to…	**Haluaisin lipun …**
single (one-way)	**meno**
return (round-trip)	**meno-paluu**
first/second class	**ensimmäinen/toinen luokka**

YOUTH HOSTELS* *(retkeilymaja).* The country has a network of some 150 youth hostels, 130 of which are affiliated with the Finnish Youth Hostel Association *(Suomen Retkeilymajajärjestö, SRM).* Unlike some other countries, Finland imposes no upper age limit, despite the name, nor do you have to reach hostels under your own steam, so motorists can also use them. SRM hostels are marked by a triangular sign with the initial letters in white on a blue background. Visitors to SRM hostels should have a membership card of their national youth hostel organization; non-members are admitted, but pay a surcharge.

Is there a youth hostel nearby?	**Onko täällä lähistöllä retkeilymajaa?**

NUMBERS

0	nolla	22	kaksikymmentäkaksi
1	yksi	30	kolmekymmentä
2	kaksi	31	kolmekymmentäyksi
3	kolme	40	neljäkymmentä
4	neljä	50	viisikymmentä
5	viisi	60	kuusikymmentä
6	kuusi	70	seitsemänkymmentä
7	seitsemän	80	kahdeksankymmentä
8	kahdeksan	90	yhdeksänkymmentä
9	yhdeksän	100	sata
10	kymmenen	101	satayksi
11	yksitoista	102	satakaksi
12	kaksitoista	110	satakymmenen
13	kolmetoista	120	satakaksikymmentä
14	neljätoista	130	satakolmekymmentä
15	viisitoista	140	sataneljäkymmentä
16	kuusitoista	150	sataviisikymmentä
17	seitsemäntoista	160	satakuusikymmentä
18	kahdeksantoista	170	sataseitsemänkymmentä
19	yhdeksäntoista	180	satakahdeksankymmentä
20	kaksikymmentä	190	satayhdeksänkymmentä
21	kaksikymmentäyksi	200	kaksisataa

SOME USEFUL EXPRESSIONS

yes/no	**kyllä/ei**
please/thank you	**olkaa hyvä/kiitos**
excuse me/you're welcome	**anteeksi/ei kestä**
where/when/how	**missä/milloin/miten**
how long/how far	**kuinka kauan/kuinka kaukana**
yesterday/today/tomorrow	**eilen/tänään/huomenna**
day/week/month/year	**päivä/viikko/kuukausi/vuosi**
left/right	**vasen/oikea**
up/down	**ylös/alas**
good/bad	**hyvä/huono**
big/small	**iso/pieni**
cheap/expensive	**halpa/kallis**
hot/cold	**kuuma/kylmä**
old/new	**vanha/uusi**
open/closed	**auki/kiinni**
free (vacant)/occupied	**vapaa/varattu**
near/far	**lähellä/kaukana**
early/late	**aikainen/myöhäinen**
quick/slow	**nopea/hidas**
full/empty	**täysi/tyhjä**
easy/difficult	**helppo/vaikea**
right/wrong	**oikea/väärä**
here/there	**täällä/siellä**
Does anyone here speak English?	**Onko täällä ketään, joka puhuu englantia?**
I don't understand.	**En ymmärrä.**
Please write it down.	**Kirjoittakaa se, olkaa hyvä.**
Waiter/Waitress, please.	**Tarjoilija/Neiti, olkaa hyvä.**
I'd like...	**Haluaisin...**
How much is that?	**Paljonko se maksaa?**
Have you something less expensive?	**Onko teillä mitään halvempaa?**
What time is it?	**Paljonko kello on?**
Just a minute.	**Hetkinen.**
Help me, please.	**Auttakaa minua.**

Index

An asterisk (*) next to a page number indicates a map reference. For index to Practical Information, see inside front cover.

All sites listed are given in their English equivalents. Finnish names are put in brackets only where the Finnish figures by itself on the maps.

059/008 SUDP 16